LIFE
BEYOND
LIVING

LIFE
BEYOND
LIVING

STEVE DAPPER and ALEX KENDRICK

B&H
PUBLISHING GROUP
NASHVILLE, TENNESSEE

978-1-4336-8480-7

Published by B&H Publishing Group
Nashville, Tennessee

Dewey Decimal Classification: 248.84
Subject Heading: CHRISTIAN LIFE \ LIFE \
HAPPINESS

1 2 3 4 5 6 7 8 • 20 19 18 17 16 15

Steve dedicates this book to his
beautiful daughters, Alana and Ashlynn.
You are my legacy.

CONTENTS

Acknowledgments

From Alex:

Without Christ, I am nothing. He is my drive, my salvation, and my Lord. May He be glorified.

I am grateful to my wife, Christina, and my children, Joshua, Anna, Catherine, Joy, Caleb, and Julia. I love you and pray God continues to mold your hearts to love and serve Him.

To my parents, Larry and Rhonwyn, and my brothers, Shannon and Stephen, who continue to support and love me. I am closer to God because of you. I am forever grateful for your influence.

Many thanks to B&H, who continue to be encouragers, partners, and friends. You have been a blessing!

FROM STEVE:

First and foremost, I would like to thank Jesus, my Lord and Savior. I am forever grateful for His love, salvation, and blessings on my life. He has shown me grace abundantly.

Thank you to my beautiful wife, Janet. You are my greatest encouragement. Thank you for not letting me quit when I wanted to give up. Thank you for your unwavering love and loyalty to me and to God through this process and through life.

Thank you to my girls, Alana and Ashlynn. I pray that this book will encourage you as God prepares you for your own life beyond living.

Thank you to my advanced readers Reid Mathis, Susan Sanders, Timothy Birney, Darius Arnold, and Tim Suddreth, who suffered through the very rough first drafts of this book. All of you are spiritual heroes in my life.

Thank you to Devin Maddox and the team at B&H Publishing Group for helping to bring this to life. You are a joy to work with.

PREFACE

I still remember, in the summer of 2009, when Steve Dapper first explained to me the concepts you are about to read in this book. We were having our regular accountability meeting at a local restaurant and asking each other the hard questions all men should be asked: "How is your marriage?" "How is your time with God?" "Are you struggling with anything?" These, along with a few more questions, have helped keep us accountable and wise. I strongly believe everyone needs at least one accountability partner.

Out of curiosity I asked Steve a question I had not asked before, "What's the most recent thing God has taught you?"

Steve's response actually impressed me very much. He began telling me that he believed the Lord had given him insight into how a man (or woman) could better understand their specific purpose in life, based on a few biblical principles that related to where God had positioned them. As an engineer, he drew a structure that made a lot of sense to me.

I've read many books dealing with the role God intends for each of us and how to view our individual purpose, so the basic ideas were not new to me. But the way Steve structured and presented it allowed me to see it from a perspective I had never seen before.

"Steve, how long have you been working on this?" I asked. He said he had written it down as he connected several biblical principles in recent weeks. His intention was to teach it to his wife and two daughters as a way of giving them a broader perspective on God's purpose for them.

I encouraged him to keep developing this concept and to pour more prayer, research, and time into it. Over the following year we continued to discuss it, and I became convinced that it would make an excellent book to use as a resource for people to see their invaluable role in God's design for life.

Almost three years after that first conversation and countless hours of work, prayer, and writing, the book was finished. In every way I could, I helped Steve craft the message and presentation of this material, but I admit that Steve did the heavy lifting as the person to whom God gave the idea.

Our prayer is that, after reading this book, you would have a fresh perspective on God's design and purpose for your life and that you would see the potential and value He has given you. Then we hope you pass it on to others as a resource to help those you love find a fulfilling life beyond living!

Alex Kendrick

Alex and I have been friends and accountability partners for several years. Although our personalities and talents are different, we both share a passion to share the love of Christ unapologetically and impact the world for God's glory. Alex has been a great encouragement to me, not only in the writing of this book, but also in life. I firmly believe part of God's design for life is that we share it with others, and I am grateful for friends like Alex in my life.

The base concepts presented in this book came from my own personal study of God's Word. He has been faithful to reveal Himself through Scripture and through my personal life experiences. While many of the connections between these concepts and certain passages of Scripture were a result of discussions Alex and I had, all of the personal references in the book are solely from my life.

God has done great things in my life, and my prayer is that He will show Himself mighty in your life as well. I hope this book will serve as a catalyst for you to strive for a deeper understanding of God's character and His plan for you. I pray that He will direct you to a purpose beyond what you could have imagined and a life beyond living.

Steve Dapper

INTRODUCTION

What is life? Webster's dictionary lists more than fifteen variations of meaning for the word *life*. It can simply mean existence, or it can be used to describe a state of being opposite of death, but the way we use the term *life* in our society necessitates that it mean something more. Life must include an inherent reason for being. It must be something beyond just existence. As you read this book, you will soon learn that life can and should include a sense of fulfillment and satisfaction.

The United States was founded on the principle that every person is entitled to the right to life, liberty, and the pursuit of happiness. Fundamentally we know that life is something to be valued and treasured. We flippantly use terms like "get a life" or "starting a new chapter in life" but often fail to ponder and reconcile for ourselves the rich meaning of the word.

In its simplest form the term *life* is what all people have in common. It spans across racial, age, and social boundaries. It includes a wide range of emotions and experiences. It offers the opportunity for success, failure, fulfillment, emptiness, and so much more. Defining the word *life* and what it means for you requires moments of deep thought, but the risk of not defining the word often yields a mere existence without really living to your fullest potential.

From the lonely old woman who fills her day with soap operas to the young teenage boy who joins a gang to satisfy his need to belong are endless examples of people who exist but don't really have life. Technology has enabled us to slip into a fog of daily routines without the necessity of engaging our brains to think through life. We can have a social network without ever speaking to anyone or leaving our homes. We can consume our free time with movies on demand, unlimited television shows, and virtual worlds we control. As the machines of today's technology are becoming more like humans, humans in our culture are becoming more like machines. We are going through the motions on a daily basis with few, if any, days of feeling alive. There must be more.

There is more.

Instinctively we know that life must have a meaning and a purpose. It is more than just our routine tasks or the pursuit of fame and fortune. It is who we are and what we do. Life in that context is what sets us apart from plants or animals. It defines us as a human race and as individuals that are unique and purposeful.

We are different from one another in our viewpoints and opinions, but most of us take interest in pursuing a satisfying life. Whether atheist or religious, young or old, student or scholar, our beliefs about the world around us define what we perceive as life and set the boundaries for how we find satisfaction and fulfillment.

As complex and sometimes difficult as life is, this life from individual conception to death is the only one we have, and in the grand scheme of things, it is relatively short. Since life is a limited and priceless resource, we should make the most of it.

I have sought and studied for a long time to try to understand life and the structure that makes it something beyond just existence. I believe it is my responsibility to understand the meaning of life so I can live my life to the fullest. It is my responsibility to understand what life is really about so I can pass down what I have learned to my children. It is my responsibility to help my children pursue the most meaningful life they can have.

It is your responsibility as well to understand the meaning of your life for yourself and for the next generation. I don't believe anyone has all the answers to life's questions, but I do believe you can use the principles in this book to discover your individual purpose and fuel your passion for life. I believe you can use the truth in these pages to help set a path toward living a fulfilling life and to find your purpose and accomplish it. You can have life beyond living.

Chapter

1

THE STRUCTURE
OF LIFE

It's true; men don't like to stop and ask for directions. My guess is that most women don't like to ask for directions either, but they are more likely to move past the pride barriers that will keep an average man heading in the wrong direction for miles. Even when we're not behind the wheel, we generally don't like to admit that we don't know where we're going. We want to feel smart and confident. We convince ourselves we don't need directions and we don't need instructions. We're smart enough to figure out how to connect the DVD player to the TV; after all, it's only a few wires. Some of the latest electronic devices don't even come with an instruction manual. Why? Because we are smart people; we can figure it out for ourselves. Or can we?

What about life? It shouldn't be hard, but oftentimes it is. We should be smart enough to navigate life without asking for directions. We should be able to figure it out, right?

That is what we tell ourselves. The problem is that many people struggle with it. They settle with the hand they have been dealt, or worse yet, they believe they have it figured out but then discover they were wrong. Some have given up trying to find meaning in life and have settled for mere existence; the daily routine is the routine of the day. The passion has died and the dreams are gone. Joy is found in small samples few and far between.

The truth is that life can be rough. I think all of us have experienced times when we feel lost; it's a part of life. Hopelessness for a season often helps our character grow, but a lifetime of hopelessness can be an insurmountable burden.

If life had an instruction manual, would we even look at it? Would we carefully study it? Would we consult it before a major decision? Would we refer to it when we hit a snag, or would we just use it as a last resort when we hit rock bottom? Would we use it to answer some of life's more daunting questions?

What should I believe?

Why am I here?

What is my purpose?

Does my life matter?

How can I find happiness?

There are too many deep questions that need answered and not enough time to discover all of the right answers for ourselves. The truth is we need a guide. We need directions for life. We need an instruction manual.

If such a book existed, wouldn't it be the most popular book in the history of the world? Wouldn't it be the best-selling book of all time? Wouldn't it be desperately sought after by those who accepted it and sharply criticized by those who rejected it?

The answer to all of these questions is yes. The book exists. It meets all of these criteria and more. The Author of the book is the Author of life. It is the Word of God, Holy Scripture, the Bible.

It makes perfect sense when you think about it: if God created us, then He must have a purpose and plan for our lives. Why would He hide that? If He expects us to think and act according to a standard, He can't expect us to know what that standard is unless He tells us.

He does.

The Bible contains the pattern for a successful life, but it doesn't come in the form of a list of rules. There are no pictures or sequential steps of assembly. There is no easy setup guide. Instead the Bible uses forms of teaching, stories and poetry that may seem difficult at first to translate into life application. The Bible has no quick-fix solutions, but it does offer some clear principles that can help you answer life's questions if you are willing to look.

The purpose of this book is to help you see and apply some of the key concepts of Scripture. It won't give you all of the answers in a week, but it can be used as a road map toward a better understanding of life, a life that God intends for us to live.

In John 10:1–18, Jesus declares Himself to be the good Shepherd to the people. John 10:10 states, "The thief comes only to steal and kill and destroy; I have come that they may have life, and have it to the full."

We already know that the thief here is Satan, and we definitely don't want what he has to offer. But what about Jesus' offer? Does that describe your life? Are you living life "to the full"? The phrase can also be translated "abundantly" or "extraordinary." Can those words describe your life? If not, then it is worth taking a look at what the Bible says about life and how God intends for us to live it.

In order to examine what the Bible says about life, we first need to create a manageable picture to represent the structure of life. In your mind visualize a building. It can be a house, an office building, or a skyscraper. Any structure with walls, windows, and doors will do. You instinctively know your building did not appear or evolve by a random collection of steel, concrete, and hardware. First a design must have been prepared, and then a founda-  tion was poured. The foundation was followed by a frame, then a covering, and then trim work. Each step in the process was built on the previous. Ultimately the result is a building that was constructed for a purpose.

Life follows a similar pattern. Just as your building must have had a design in order to fulfill a purpose, our lives are also designed to fulfill a purpose. Just as your building must have had a solid foundation to stand, our lives must also have a solid foundation on which we base our beliefs, motives, and character.

The unique difference between the building you imagined and your life is choice. In life you choose the foundation. You choose the building blocks that affect your circumstances and define you as a person.

As we think about the choice of foundation, we start with the basics. We master the basic principles of math before progressing into algebra, calculus, and differential equations. In music we become skilled with the basic notes and rhythm before performing songs and symphonies.

In this book we will take a similar approach to life. We will define the basic principles that govern life and how those principles become the foundation to form the structure, which leads us to the purpose of life. By developing an understanding of the basic principles, we can gain enormous insight into how life works, how to find purpose in life, and what we must change in our lives in order to be successful.

Inherently people share a common goal of success. We want success at work, in our families, and in life; but have you ever stopped to think about what success means? Our culture makes much of success, or at least what we think is success. We follow the lives of movie stars and athletes, sometimes longing for a similar type of life. We want that illusive "lucky break" that will launch us into fame and fortune. We desire the lifestyle that always seems out of reach. But is that really what life is about? Do fame and fortune bring happiness in life? Is success really quantified in dollars or media attention? The answer to all of these questions is no. "He who works his land will have abundant food, but he who chases fantasies lacks judgment" (Prov. 12:11).

Let's take a closer look at that building you imagined. Throughout this book we will look first at the right foundation on which we build our lives. Once we have a firm foundation, we will look at the building blocks that are set on that foundation to form a meaningful structure. We will dedicate a chapter to each of these building blocks to help you understand how they support the abundant life Christ refers to in John 10:10.

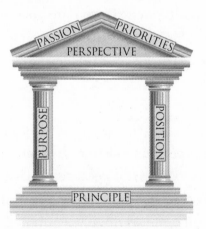

PRINCIPLE

A foundational principle is a fundamental truth or law upon which others are based. Your principles are the set of laws and guidelines that define who you are and what you believe. Similar to the laws of physics or the laws of nature, the truths you believe are based on a principle that sets the standard to govern everything about your life. Your foundational principle should align with your own individual character, and it is the basis for your attitudes, behaviors, reactions, and styles. It is the foundation of your life.

Discovering and understanding the foundational principle that will define you is essential to finding your purpose and will dictate the legacy you leave behind. What your children remember about you and what people say about you after you are gone will be more focused on your character than your accomplishments. Character is driven by your principle.

POSITION

Everyone's position is defined by their principle. You are where you are partly because of what you believe to be true. Position is your location physically, emotionally, relationally, and spiritually. Position defines where you are and sets the direction for where you are going.

PURPOSE

Purpose is linked to position and principle. Your purpose is the fulfillment of your life design. Purpose is the reason you are here. If you choose to pour your life into your job, then you will feel most fulfilled when you reach a milestone in your career or have a successful, work-related achievement. Your purpose becomes to move higher in the corporate world, to gain more power, or to get the next promotion.

If you believe your purpose is to help others, you will likely find that your position is in the medical or service field, or you may find yourself volunteering for community work. Position and purpose are closely linked. To fulfill your purpose, you need to be in the right place at the right time.

PASSION

Once your principle is settled, your position is known, and your purpose is defined, your passions can be used to help you find joy in fulfilling your purpose.

Our passions are the driving force behind what we really desire to do. A sailboat follows the laws of physics to stay afloat and fulfills a purpose in motion, but wind enables the boat to sail. Passion is like the wind. It drives us to fulfill our purpose.

PERSPECTIVE

Our perspective is how we view our place in the world. Position defines our location, but perspective is the view from that location. Most people who sign up for television talent show auditions believe themselves to be the next great singer, dancer, or entertainer. Their perspective depends on a principle heavily weighted toward success in the field of entertainment. For some it becomes the most important goal in life. Their purpose is to demonstrate their talents with the hope of a future position of fame. You may think you are one of those "undiscovered divas," or you may view yourself as insignificant and worthless. Both of those extremes are incorrect. Basing your perspective on the right principle will bring your viewpoint back down to reality and let you perform in life at your own personal capability.

PRIORITIES

A good understanding of our principle, position, and purpose should also lead to prioritization of our lives. Priority means setting some things as a greater value than others. Priorities must not only be based on principle, position, and purpose but must be kept in check with these structure blocks. To ensure that you are leaving the legacy you want to leave for those around you, your priorities should reflect your principle.

In journalism, reporters are taught to ask who, what, where, why, when, and how. Those questions define the story being reported. Those questions can also help define our lives. We should ask those questions from both a collective and an individual perspective. The *who* is principle. Our principle defines who we are. Who are you right now, and who do you want to be? The *where* is position. Where are we as a society, and where are you as an individual? The *why* is purpose. What is your purpose, and what is the purpose of humankind? The *when* is priority. Once you know what you should be doing, how do you prioritize your time and resources to maximize the efficiency of your purpose? Finally, the *how* is passion. Fulfilling your purpose can be accomplished in a variety of ways. Which of those ways caters most to your individual desires and inclinations? The perspective is your point of view.

Each of these *P* words represents a critical concept of life that we will expand throughout this book. Collectively these concepts form a well-structured, purposeful life—a life "to the full."

Our modern culture leaves little time for reflection on these concepts. The fast pace of society and the bombardment of media messages can force us to continue going through the motions without stopping to think about life. We can easily get caught up in keeping up with information, technology, events, and fads without developing and understanding how we as individuals can impact the world and one another.

I don't have all of the answers to life's questions, but I do know that defining these concepts has helped keep my life and my legacy in perspective. These concepts have also helped me live a satisfying life. My wife and I have been blessed with two rapidly growing girls. This book began as a way for me to help teach my girls what I have learned about how life works. My hope is that anyone who reads this will better understand these critical concepts of life and that a better understanding of life will lead to a more fulfilled life. The remaining chapters of this book will explore the practical application of each of these concepts and provide some guidance on how they fit in to the base principle that leads to a life beyond living.

Dan's Story

Throughout this book we will look at the story of Dan, an ordinary guy not much different from you or me. We will use Dan to illustrate some of the concepts in this book in a real-life context.

Dan is a nice guy. He grew up in an average, middle-class home and was characterized as being quiet and shy. He was a good student through both high school and college, but didn't fit into any of the popular social circles. He survived school with a small group of friends, but his lack of self-confidence led him to keep mostly to himself.

Dan started his work experience mowing lawns in the neighborhood and took on some after-school jobs during high school. When he started college, Dan took a night job loading delivery trucks to pay for tuition and books. He was a hard worker and fast learner, but Dan was somewhat troubled by something that appeared to be missing. He struggled with the meaning of his life. Sure, the purpose of his job was to pay for school, and the purpose of his school was to get a better job, but to what end? Was life really just about having a good job and making a lot of money? Dan found himself struggling with these questions as many of us struggle with these questions. Some of Dan's friends moved away or went on road trips to "find themselves," but since they couldn't really explain what they were looking for, Dan concluded there must be a better way to answer some of these deep life questions.

Chapter

2

PRINCIPLE
CHARACTERISTICS

Principle, by definition, is "a fundamental law or truth from which others are derived." It is the basis for your thought processes, behavior patterns, and interactions. It is the foundation of the building and establishes the foundation of your life. What you believe has a profound impact on your behavior, and your behavior over time defines how people view your character. Because your principle is such a critical factor in determining the structure of life, committing to a principle should be well thought-out.

Whether they know it or not, everyone already has a foundational principle by which they are living life. We make choices and decisions based on what we believe to be true; however, a principle doesn't necessarily need to be true to make it convincing or believable.

When my youngest daughter was two years old, she believed a strong wind could lift her off the ground and blow her far away. Her misdirected belief caused her to be extremely upset and fearful about a force of nature we knew was harmless. Although we're not sure where she developed this principle, we knew she was convinced of it. On any given windy day, she would hold my hand or latch on to my leg like her life depended on it. The panic and anxiety were clear on her face and impacted her behavior. Thankfully she grew out of that stage, and her principle regarding the power of the wind changed into a more reasonable belief.

I remember in my own life being self-conscious about how my peers viewed me during the critical middle-school and high-school years. I made several attempts to say the cool things and wear the cool clothes because that is what I thought was important in life. Ultimately, none of those attempts brought me any closer to sitting with the popular kids at lunch or gave me a real purpose in life.

It has been amazing to me to watch both of my girls develop their own principle about life based on what they are learning as they grow up. Every lesson helps them understand their principle better. Sometimes they need to adjust their thoughts or behaviors to line up with what they know their principle should be. Sometimes I need to calibrate my thoughts or actions against my principle as well.

Every discipline of education originates from a principle. Scientifically, everything we examine has a basis from the laws of nature and physics. All equations are based on mathematic theorems. Two plus two always equals four. That fact needs to hold true in order to hold up the structure of the entire mathematical process. The same holds true in the study of medicine, law, and finance. Each of these fields has a unique structure based on a set of base principles. Life also has a structure and, for life to have meaning, it must be based on a principle. Some basic truths must be foundational to our beliefs. These truths influence our view of the world. These truths become our principle.

There are many common principles in our culture today. These are sometimes referred to as worldviews. Commonly accepted principles can take the form of popular religious texts such as the Bible, the Qur'an, and The Book of Mormon as well as nonreligious ideologies. Each principle should be examined to ensure it is consistent, time-tested, universally applicable, understandable, and sensible.

CONSISTENCY

Many people either knowingly or unknowingly base their foundational principle on their own philosophies and thoughts. The inherit danger in having a principle based on personal philosophy is the lack of consistency. Just as what I thought would make me cool as a young teenager and just as what my daughter believed about the wind when she was young, what you think or believe today without a strong principle basis may change five to ten years from now.

Have you ever made a decision you regretted later? I think most of us have. In this fast-paced life too often we don't consider the consequences or permanence of our choices. Most of us know of at least one person in our lives who made a decision that resulted in lifelong consequences.

Growth and maturity change our outlook on life. Major events in life can change our perspectives and priorities. The personal perspective and priorities for Steve Dapper changed radically when I met and married my wife. Those perspectives and priorities changed again at the birth of our first daughter and changed yet again when our second daughter was born. Each of these events expanded my purpose in the world. Suddenly I was a husband when I had not been a husband before. Then I became a father for the first time. My responsibilities in life increased. My position changed, and it altered my priorities and purpose. Changes such as these required that I have a consistent and universal principle to govern my life. To operate under my own set of ideologies based on experience may have worked prior to getting married, but once I made those vows to my wife and signed the marriage certificate, my unmarried principles became insufficient.

When I became a father, I had no previous personal experience to know what I should and should not do. I could no longer rely solely on my own notions of right and wrong but instead needed to resort to a solid principle that addressed all of the phases of my life—the way I should behave as a single adult, the way I should behave as a husband, and the way I should behave as a father. I couldn't have developed those on my own. Without prior knowledge and experience any self-initiated principle would have been shallow and inconsistent at best.

I have found that most people crave consistency of character. My wife knows my demeanor and has confidence she won't see huge fluctuations in my attitudes, thoughts, and reactions. The more consistent I am, the less anxiety she has about our relationship. She doesn't need to worry about me yelling at her or punching holes in the wall when I am upset; it is not in my character to do so. I am certainly capable of letting my emotions get out of control, but the principle I have chosen to live by consistently governs my character. I know how I should react based on my principle, and I choose to control my attitudes and reactions accordingly.

Consistency in character often yields consistency in action. We categorize people as "nice" or "mean" based on the consistency of their character. We expect nice people to act nice, and we aren't surprised when mean people act mean. A solid principle can help drive both consistencies in character and in action.

When our girls were babies, they followed a consistent schedule. They slept at certain times, ate at certain times, and played at certain times. Even though they couldn't read a clock, their bodies adjusted to a consistent and predictable schedule. That consistency helped produce well-behaved children. Any deviation from that consistent schedule yielded opposite results.

Since consistency is critical to principle and given that our own thought processes change so much as we mature, the principle we use to define the purpose in life needs to be something more than what we personally determine are the guidelines to live by. Similar to the laws of nature and physics, our principle should be time-tested and consistently true.

TIME-TESTED

Even before Sir Isaac Newton published his *Mathematical Principles of Natural Philosophy* in 1687, the law of gravity was a time-tested principle throughout time. Earlier civilizations may not have understood the details of why it worked, but they knew that the law of gravity was at work on broken trees, rain clouds, and their own bodies after a stumble. The law of gravity is both time-tested and consistent. The same can be said for many laws of physics, mathematics, and nature. We feel confident in events, occasions, or cycles of nature that have been verified over time. We rely on many of these time-verified events to survive. Because of nature's predictability, we know when to plant crops, when to harvest, when to fish, when to work, and when to sleep. We don't feel uncertainty or anxiety about these principles. The same should hold true for the principle that governs life.

UNIVERSALLY APPLICABLE

Principles can unknowingly be inherited. People often follow the beliefs of their family or surrounding community without questioning their authenticity. How many people commit to a parenting style that was different than the one they were raised in? Yet oftentimes those same people become just like their own parents. Without a valid principle to help govern their parenting style, the way they were raised becomes the default. It is all they know.

There are inherent risks when you adopt the principle of those around you. Following the "accepted" principle of your community or your family places the influential control for your life in the hands of the community or family. If you adopt an untested principle, your family may have no provision for how you should react in certain uncharted circumstances. For example, if you discover that your unborn baby has a serious mental illness, then you may be at a loss when the doctor delivers the bad news. What should you do? No one in your family has ever had to deal with such a circumstance so there is no point of reference. How do you know that the community principle offers the best direction on what to do in this situation? What does your principle say about issues such as abortion or euthanasia? If you don't have a predetermined and universal position on these issues, you may not know what to do. Your decisions in certain circumstances become a reflection on your character and on your legacy so you cannot risk making the wrong choice. When faced with a difficult situation, no one wants to be forced to make a decision based on the emotional environment at the time, but without another option there may be a lot of room for regret.

Mimicking the principle of the community without taking the time to invest in understanding and internalizing that principle in your own life can result in your feeling out of control. The decisions you make will be directed by someone else's view or belief system instead of you own.

Are you willing to trust the direction of your life to someone else? Perhaps the predominant principle in your community is the correct one, but how do you know? Without a significant level of research, thought, and reasoning, you may not.

Life is made up of choices. Choices are based on reasons, and those reasons are based on principle. My girls will have many choices to make in life. I don't want them to repeat a lot of the mistakes I made early in life so I hope they base their decisions on their understanding of their own principle instead of just doing what those before them would have done. To ensure they make the right decisions, I need to make sure they understand their principle for themselves. Since purpose in life is defined by principle, the stakes are too high to rely on the philosophies of others without reconciling the right principle for your own life.

UNDERSTANDABLE

Choosing the right principle is important, but almost as important is the understanding of why that principle is right for you. You'll have a much stronger sense of loyalty to a principle when you have researched and developed an understanding of why you believe what you believe. Without that basic understanding you will likely be at a loss when a circumstance arises that is not specifically addressed by your principle or when you are confronted with an opposing view of life.

I am a strong advocate of your understanding what you know. I do my best to drive this point home with my girls in their schoolwork. It just isn't enough to memorize the answers, take the test, and move on. They need to have a level of intellectual growth. The definition of a word can be memorized and recited, but to understand what it really means, you must use it in a sentence.

The same is true for principle. You can memorize a list of guidelines and rules, but an entirely different and deeper level of commitment takes place when you understand the guidelines and then practice them in daily life. Understanding why you believe what you believe leads to more secure and confident decision-making when the choices of life arise.

SENSIBLE

The fundamental truths of a principle also need to make sense. Several popular principles in our society seem illogical. For example, universalism claims that all religions are true, yet several religions teach opposing ideologies that cannot possibly be reconciled. Some philosophies claim "there is no absolute truth," but that very statement negates itself. If there is no absolute truth, then the statement that "there is no absolute truth" cannot possibly be absolutely true. The commonsense test must be one of the first tests applied when looking at the right principle for life. It is not necessary that you understand every detailed aspect of the principle, but you must research enough to reconcile for yourself that it is truth.

A great principle should be consistent, time-tested, universally applicable, understandable, and sensible.

The reason these parameters are so critical is that principle really defines the basis for what is right and what is wrong in our lives. The analysis of your thoughts or actions needs to be based against some type of standard. That standard will govern your thoughts, beliefs, attitudes, and actions. It will also define your position, purpose, passion, perspective, and priorities. In essence it is the design of your life, and this is the only life you have. There is a lot to take into consideration and a lot of possibilities to choose from, but in order to find purpose and to live a fulfilling life, it is necessary to contemplate and research to find the principle that is fundamentally solid.

The step of researching and choosing the right principle for your life is the first step toward life legacy. Leaving a legacy of doing the right thing means taking responsibility for the choices you make. It is a responsibility we expect from others, and it is one we should expect of ourselves. If you drop your wallet in a store, would you expect that whoever found it would do the right thing and contact you or turn it in to the store management? If you found a dent in your car in the parking lot, would you expect to find a note on the windshield with an apology and some contact information? If you take your car to the shop to get it fixed, would you expect to be treated fairly and honestly? We expect others to have the right principle and to do the right thing when it impacts our lives so we should also expect the same behavior of ourselves. The question is: Do you have the right principle to ensure that you will do the right thing for others?

Dan's Story

When Dan was young, he went to church with his family. He knew enough about heaven and hell to recognize that he didn't want to go to hell when he died. When he was young, Dan prayed the normal church prayer that would keep him out of hell. Not much celebration followed that event. It seemed to be just a natural part of growing up, like learning to ride a bike. Still it seemed to meet the expectations of those around him so Dan continued through his life just as he had been doing.

When he entered high school, Dan noticed that something wasn't right. He had been taught that hard work and sticking to the right moral standard would result in happiness and blessings, but that wasn't what he saw. In fact, it looked like the rich kids who didn't care much about hard work or any moral standards were getting more than their fair share of happiness and blessings. Dan's dad was a hard worker, but his family couldn't afford the latest fashion or the nicest car. Things just weren't adding up. This was the principle Dan grew up believing, but he felt like something was missing. The more Dan thought about what he believed, the more questions he had.

Without a solid understanding of his principle, life put Dan to the test. On a cold, rainy day Dan was backing his car out of the mall parking lot. Without realizing, he turned too sharp and scraped the car next to his. He stopped and looked around. No one saw him, and the rainfall started getting heavy. It wasn't a huge mark, but how big was too big? Dan's car also had a mark, but it wasn't bad, and he was planning on getting a new paint job soon anyway. Should he try to contact the owner of the car, or is this just a common parking-lot mishap people expect to happen? If he left a note, it would just get soaked and would probably be illegible. Ultimately, Dan convinced himself to flee. That is what car insurance is for, right? No one needed to know.

Dan got his car fixed and newly painted. A few months later a drunk driver ran through a red light and hit Dan's car, ripping the front bumper off. The drunk driver sped off, leaving Dan in the middle of the intersection and his bumper on the side of the road. Irony.

Chapter

3

THE ESTABLISHED
PRINCIPLE

We have already seen how a self-developed principle or a community principle may not be the wisest choice to offer a satisfying life so now let's look at some principles that have been established throughout history. Most established principles follow a basic pattern that guides you to do the right thing.

Our conscience provides us with a sense of right or wrong and most often an urge to do what is right. This natural sense of right and wrong permeates common law and governed law throughout the world, which leads us to ask the question, "Could there be one overriding principle that most other principles are based on?"

To answer that question, we need to look at some of the oldest archeological finds in history regarding common or governed law. One of the oldest records of government law is the Code of Hammurabi, dating back to the era of 1750 BC. Hammurabi was the ruler of Babylon from 1792 BC to 1750 BC. The code contained about three hundred laws carved on an upright stone tablet and was discovered during an archeological expedition in AD 1901. The code addressed legal matters, business contracts, and issues regarding family relationships. Several of the laws on the stone and the manner in which they are written are similar to biblical laws found in the Old Testament books of Exodus, Leviticus, and Deuteronomy. For example, the phrase "eye for an eye" can be found in both the Hammurabi Code and in Exodus 21:24. The Hammurabi Code and the similarities found in the Old Testament establish that a common-law principle was prevalent in ancient times.[1]

Many of the behavioral principles we teach our children are taken from ancient religious or common-law principles. The Golden Rule states that we should treat others in the manner we want to be treated. This guideline for life can be found in the records of ancient Babylon, China, Egypt, and Greece. The Golden Rule was also established as the common principle for many religions by the Council for a Parliament of the World's Religions. This group has been in existence since AD 1893 and seeks harmony among the world's religions. The Golden Rule is commonly attributed to the teachings of Jesus Christ in Matthew 7:12 but can also be credited to two Old Testament verses in Leviticus 19:18 and Leviticus 19:34.

As seen throughout history, a common law, or life principle, is not a new idea. Individuals, communities, and nations have sought to promote a set of standards for people to live a responsible and satisfying life. Often these established principles are validated by our own conscience and become the basis for a civilized society.

The most popular established principles are those taking the form of religious texts. Some of these texts have been in existence for centuries while others have only been established within the past few hundred years. In terms of sheer numbers, the Bible is by far the front-runner. The Bible tops the best-seller list every year without fail. In fact, it has dominated the charts so much that it is considered a perennial and is no longer listed on the best-seller list on a regular basis. Nearly

100 million Bibles are sold every year. It has been translated into more than three thousand languages and is the most researched and talked about book in the world. With more than six billion copies sold, the Bible is the top-selling book of all time.[2]

Numerous books have been written on the validity and power of the Bible, and the amount of research that has been done regarding the legitimacy of the Bible is astounding. It is among the oldest books of history and has survived multiple attempts at extinction. In AD 303 the Roman emperor Diocletian ordered the destruction of all Scripture and the persecution of Christians. Within ten years of that edict, Diocletian died, and fifteen years later the Roman emperor Constantine declared Christianity the official religion of the Roman Empire. There have been various historical attempts to destroy the Bible, which have all been met with failure.

The Bible declares itself to be indestructible: "The grass withers and the flowers fall, but the word of our God stands forever" (Isa. 40:8).

The Bible contains archeologically validated facts and deep wisdom for life. Although penned by more than forty different authors over sixteen hundred years, it is consistent within itself and declares itself to be inspired by a holy and omnipotent God. "Above all, you must understand that no prophecy of Scripture came about by the prophet's own interpretation. For prophecy never had its origin in the will of man, but men spoke from God as they were carried along by the Holy Spirit" (2 Pet. 1:20–21).

Many have attempted and failed to prove that the Bible is incorrect, and it continues to spread a message of hope and salvation across nations, continents, and cultures.

In addition to its time-tested consistency, the Bible is one of few texts that defines itself as the Word of God and declares itself to be the principle upon which life should be based. "He humbled you, causing you to hunger and then feeding you with manna, which neither you nor your fathers had known, to teach you that man does not live on bread alone but on every word that comes from the mouth of the LORD" (Deut. 8:3).

This verse is taken from the address Moses gave to the Israelites while they camped in the wilderness. God wanted to teach the Israelites that man should not survive off physical sustenance alone, but instead they should live "on every word that comes from the mouth of the LORD." In our world today that word "from the mouth of the Lord" is the Bible.

Life is much more than survival. Our purpose is greater than survival. We can sustain existence by food and water alone, but we cannot truly live a completely satisfying life without fulfilling our purpose.

The Bible stands as the only revelation of Jesus Christ as Lord. It also declares itself as the true life principle above any other principle: "See to it that no one takes you captive through hollow and deceptive philosophy, which depends on human tradition and the basic principles of this world rather than on Christ" (Col. 2:8).

Paul wrote this verse to the church in the city of Colosse, which was located in present-day Turkey. The church had a strong foundation but was being enticed by other principles including the worship of angels and prescribed rituals. Hollow and deceptive philosophy can be alluring but can be dispelled quickly with adequate research. Paul warns them that any principle that relies on traditions or the basic rules of the world rather than on Christ would leave them with less than total fulfillment. That warning also holds true for us today.

In addition to the Bible's declaration of itself as the only true life principle, it also declares itself to be complete and correct: "All Scripture is God-breathed and is useful for teaching, rebuking, correcting and training in righteousness, so that the man of God may be thoroughly equipped for every good work" (2 Tim. 3:16–17).

In the book of Deuteronomy, Moses gives the Israelites some final instructions before they enter into the land God promised them. In his address to the people, Moses said: "Take to heart all the words I have solemnly declared to you this day, so that you may command your children to obey carefully all the words of this law. They are not just idle words for you—they are your life" (Deut. 32:46–47).

Can the Bible really hold the key to a fulfilling and satisfying life? Can this book contain the direction to find a rich life beyond just existence?

I believe the following pages of this book will answer that question with a resounding yes.

Over any other principle the Bible meets and exceeds the requirements for a solid foundation in life. It is easy enough for children to understand its basic concepts, yet complex enough to be studied by scholars. It is independent of tradition and the principles of the community. It provides the reader with a perspective on life that was written by the original Designer of life. The Bible provides us with our principle, position, and purpose. It directs us in our perspective, priorities, and passions.

With this chapter I only scratch the surface of the evidence for the validity of the Bible as our established principle. Please don't just take my word for it. Research it. Study it. Based on your own thorough research, discover and decide for yourself. Ultimately, God is the Creator of our life and Designer of our purpose. He wants us to seek Him and promises that if we do, we will find Him. He sets before us a choice and makes known His recommendation. Life or death, blessings or curses. "This day I call heaven and earth as witnesses against you that I have set before you life and death, blessings and curses. Now choose life, so that you and your children may live and that you may love the LORD your God, listen to his voice, and hold fast to him" (Deut. 30:19–20).

Make your choice.

Dan's Story

Dan's questions about how life worked and about what he really believed stuck with him for many years. Dan had been taught that the Bible was true and had just accepted it as a fact for much of his young life. Eventually, Dan came to a crossroad in life that spurred him to do some research. He was determined to find the truth for himself. He studied the Bible and compared it with other religious texts and organizations. He also compared the Bible with what he thought he knew about God and Christianity. The more he studied, the more he found stories and concepts in the Bible that have been validated in history. Honestly, some passages in the Bible didn't fit the paradigm he grew up with and didn't seem to make sense with his understanding of God and Christianity. He welcomed questions that challenged him to dig deeper and set his own foundation for his beliefs. He began to realize there was much more to this book than he had been taught to believe. At first this was a bit surprising. In the environment Dan grew up in, the Bible was primarily a list of rules to follow and sins to avoid. The more he studied, the more enlightened he became concerning the real purpose of the Bible. This led Dan to a startling conclusion.

4

THE PRINCIPLE
FOUNDATION

C an a book really provide the answer to questions of life? Can it offer the only real principle for a purposeful and fulfilling life? The answer is surprisingly simple. Take a look at this psalm and note the different descriptors for the Word of God ("law," "testimonies," "precepts," "statutes," "commandments," "judgments"):

> Blessed are they whose way is blameless, who walk in the law of the LORD. Blessed are they

who keep his statutes and seek him with all their heart. They do nothing wrong; they walk in his ways. You have laid down precepts that are to be fully obeyed. Oh, that my ways were steadfast in obeying your decrees! Then I would not be put to shame when I consider all your commands. I will praise you with an upright heart as I learn your righteous laws. I will obey your decrees; do not utterly forsake me.

How can a young man keep his way pure? By living according to Your word. (Ps. 119:1–9 NASB)

Each of these descriptors has a unique application on our lives. The word *blessed* translates "happy" or "satisfied." From this psalm, we can be blessed if:

- Our walk (daily direction) is in the law of the Lord.
- Our obedience and observation are to His Word.
- Our motivation (passion) is to seek Him further.

If we accept the Bible as our foundational principle, then consistently following the teachings of Scripture and seeking to understand it more becomes the driver for a satisfying life beyond mere existence. We rely on Scripture to define who we are and what our purpose in life is. In Scripture we find the priorities we should have and the passions we should be nurturing. Also in Scripture we develop a perspective on who God is and who we are in relation to Him and to one another. Everything we need is there if we are willing to look.

In Luke 6:47–49, Jesus uses a parable to explain the importance of Scripture as the only foundational principle for life:

> I will show you what he is like who comes to me and hears my words and puts them into practice. He is like a man building a house, who dug down deep and laid the foundation on rock. When a flood came, the torrent struck that house but could not shake it, because it was well built. But the one who hears my words and does not put them into practice is like a man who built a house on the ground without a foundation. The moment the torrent struck that house, it collapsed and its destruction was complete.

The parable applies not only to those who were present when Jesus spoke but also to us as we read the Bible for ourselves. It is noteworthy to see here that the man who does not practice the words of Scripture does not last long when the storms come. In the parable Jesus says that the moment the storm struck, the house fell. It was not a slow deterioration; it was a sudden collapse. This man did not have an ignorance disclaimer; he heard the message just like the man who built his house on the rock. He built a house just like the other man, and both houses felt the full force of the torrent. What the foolish man lacked was the application.

We must do more than just read the Bible; we must seek to understand and apply it. The caution here is that we don't slip into a religious habit of reading the Bible without seeking to understand and apply it in our lives. Studying Scripture and applying it to our lives result in maturity while shallow habitual reading results in hypocrisy. James, the half brother of Jesus and pastor at the first church in Jerusalem, addresses this point: "Do not merely listen to the word, and so deceive yourselves. Do what it says. Anyone who listens to the word but does not do what it says is like a man who looks at his face in a mirror and, after looking at himself, goes away and immediately forgets what he looks like. But the man who looks intently into the perfect law that gives freedom, and continues to do this, not forgetting what he has heard, but doing it—he will be blessed in what he does" (James 1:22–25).

Similar to Psalm 119, one of the key points in this passage is a path to a life that is blessed, secure, and satisfied.

Notice how Jesus describes the man who listens and practices what the Word of God says. The wise man described in this passage did several things right. He came to Jesus, heard the Word, and put the Word into practice. Not only did this man build his foundation on rock, the Bible says he "dug down deep" (Luke 6:48). Don't miss the importance of the phrase "dug deep" because it is a critical aspect of principle. Not only do we need to choose the right principle for the right reasons; we also need to study and know our principle. Many societies have no shortage of religious people but seemingly few who hunger and thirst for righteousness. God desires people in the latter category. "The LORD looks down from heaven on the sons of men to see if there are any who understand, any who seek God" (Ps. 14:2).

In the context of righteous hunger and thirst, Jesus gives His followers this promise: "Ask and it will be given to you; seek and you will find; knock and the door will be opened to you. For everyone who asks receives; he who seeks finds; and to him who knocks, the door will be opened" (Matt. 7:7–8).

This verse requires more careful study than just a casual glance. If you take this verse out of context and at face value, it can wrongfully be used to display God as some mystical genie who desires to grant our wishes.

That is not what this verse is saying at all. This verse and the corresponding verse in Luke 11 are in the context of selfless prayer requests. The words *ask, seek,* and *knock* have a much stronger action associated with them in the original Greek language. The word *ask* can also be translated "beg" or "desire." The word *seek* is not just a casual looking but seeking with a drive to find. Seeking a pair of shoes is much different from seeking the right medicine when you are sick. The word "knock" refers to a continual knocking; it is persistent and desperate. It is more accurately translated to "knock and keep knocking." The same word is used in Revelation 3:20 when Jesus says, "I stand at the door and knock."

The verse in Revelation is often used as an evangelical verse, but the context of the verse is addressing the church. It was written in a letter to the church of Laodicea just sixty years after Christ's resurrection. That in itself is a sad commentary on man's tendency to stray quickly from what God originally intended. Through His discipleship of the apostles, Jesus set up the church as a body of believers called to glorify Him through worship and commanded them to go and make disciples of all nations. Christ set the foundation of the church on Himself in Matthew 16 and gave His life for the church as recorded in Ephesians 5. Yet just a few years after Christ's departure from the earth,

Revelation 3:20 paints a picture of Jesus standing at the door of the church in Laodicea longing to enter.

Jesus then says, "If anyone hears my voice and opens the door, I will come in and eat with him, and he with me." The implication here is that He will continue to stand at the door and will keep knocking until someone hears and opens the door. This is the type of seeking Christ modeled for us, and this is the type of seeking we should have for Him and His Word. The message here is that those who claim the Bible as their foundational principle should research it and need to seek out and ask for God's revelation of their individual purpose.

This isn't about religion. Religion alone will not provide the fulfillment and purpose we long for. The principle of the Bible is much deeper. It is more about relationship. A shallow level of principle understanding comes from using the Bible as a set of rules and standards for living, but there is a deeper level of principle understanding when you can have a relationship with the Designer of your life. The verse in Revelation states that if we open the door Jesus will come in and eat with us and we with Him. This is much more than memorizing the list of right and wrong actions; it is an intimate relationship.

In your house the place to entertain guests is in the living room or family room, but the place to prepare food and dine is reserved for your closest family and friends. That is where Jesus wants to be in our lives.

You can understand a lot about a machine or a building by researching the design drawings from which it was built, but you can get a much deeper understanding by talking to the man who designed it. You can gain an even deeper level by spending enough time with the designer that you are comfortable having him or her over for dinner.

Scripture commands us to seek first His kingdom and His righteousness and promises that if we do seek His Word and His will for our lives, we will find it. The rewards are clear. "Blessed are those who hunger and thirst for righteousness, for they will be filled" (Matt. 5:6). "But seek first his kingdom and his righteousness, and all these things will be given to you as well" (Matt. 6:33).

If we seek, we will find, but it is our responsibility to seek. If we hunger and thirst, then we will be filled. If we seek His kingdom and His righteousness first, everything else (food, clothes, water, and the other necessities of life) will be provided for us. These words give security. They provide a solid foundation. They have been tested and proven countless times throughout history. Great men and women of faith have studied Scripture end- lessly with far fewer resources than we have today. These

men and women longed for an understanding of truth.
These men and women, truly seeking to understand who
God is, have a deeper understanding of who they are and
what their purpose is.

Many cultures have redefined happiness to mean
entertainment and materialism. The Bible defines *happiness* as delight in God and His Word:

> Blessed is the man who does not walk in the
> counsel of the wicked or stand in the way of sinners or sit in the seat of mockers. But his delight
> is in the law of the LORD, and on his law he
> meditates day and night. (Ps. 1:1–2)

> Praise the LORD. Blessed is the man who fears
> the LORD, who finds great delight in his commands. (Ps. 112:1)

> Then will I go to the altar of God, to God, my
> joy and my delight. I will praise you with the
> harp, O God, my God. (Ps. 43:4)

> For in my inner being I delight in God's law.
> (Rom. 7:22)

The word *delight* used here is an inward joy and satisfaction. God's word holds true as much today as when the words of Scripture were first penned. Studying the Bible should not be burdensome or boring; it should be delightful. It should become for us a sweet craving and a desire to dig deeper each time. It should stir in us a desire to mature from elementary teachings to deeper understanding.

The writer of Hebrews cautions that "though by this time you ought to be teachers, you need someone to teach you the elementary truths of God's word all over again. You need milk, not solid food! Anyone who lives on milk, being still an infant, is not acquainted with the teaching about righteousness. But solid food is for the mature, who by constant use have trained themselves to distinguish good from evil" (Heb. 5:12–14).

Our culture has fallen into this same trap. We should be much better versed in Scripture than we are. A time must come when we choose to stop being distracted or lazy. Growth is a choice. Throughout the Bible we are encouraged to strive, labor, seek, run the race, and stand firm. These are all action verbs; it takes effort but effort that has a great reward.

This is not about religious fanaticism, but instead it is about a practical application of a strong principle to define purpose. The world is full of people who claim to follow the Bible but are acting contrary to what it says. Many of these people have unknowingly created in others an aversion for the Bible with their actions. Don't let someone's opinion about the Bible be the basis for your understanding of it. You must read it for yourself to decide. Remember that the choice of principle belongs to you. Whatever principle you choose becomes the basis for fulfillment in your life in addition to your legacy.

You must choose to believe it or not. Is the Bible true? Is it really the only foundational principle to base our lives on? Is it the principle you want to build your legacy from? Does it really give you joy when you study it? The choice belongs to each individual. The choice belongs to you. "Choose for yourselves this day whom you will serve, whether the gods your forefathers served beyond the River, or the gods of the Amorites, in whose land you are living. But as for me and my household, we will serve the LORD" (Josh. 24:15).

Dan's Story

The truth was there the whole time. Dan had decided the Bible was going to be his foundational principle, but not the Bible as he understood it before. This time Dan saw the Bible as something much more than a moral code to live by. He saw characteristics, emotions, and descriptions of God. The Bible wasn't just a list of rules to follow to get to heaven; it painted a picture of who God really is. Words and verses Dan had read early in his life suddenly took on grander meaning, and all of the pieces started to fit. At first it took some effort, but soon Dan found himself wanting to read more. He wanted to dig deeper. Every time he read, he found something he didn't see before. He began to understand more and more about God's character and motives. Dan took a deeper look at the reasons God acted the way He did.

Through his study of the Bible, Dan also started to see himself in a different light. Maybe he wasn't as good as he thought he was. Maybe he knew all of the right words to say but wasn't really feeling it in his heart. Maybe the way he thought and acted when no one was watching was different from the person he let others see. While searching for a personal application to his own life, Dan was hit with a thought that brought him to his knees in tears.

Chapter

5

THE RELATIONSHIP
PRINCIPLE

R ules are everywhere. At work, at school, on the
road, at the dinner table, and at church, we
encounter lists of rules to be followed that are
considered to be proper. Most of the time, the rules in
our lives are there for a good reason. As much as I don't
always agree with the speed limit signs on my way to
work, I know the speed limit rules are intended to keep
me and others safe. I also know that deliberate disobedience to those rules can have costly consequences. As
important as some of these rules are, there is much

more to life and much more to foundational principle than a list of rules.

It would be a great fallacy to describe the Bible *only* as the set of standards and guidelines by which to govern your life. Although the Bible is the only foundational principle by which we should base our lives, choices, and behaviors, it is also much more. The Bible, more than any other religious text, provides a portrayal and depiction of who God is. Within the pages of Scripture, we find the characteristics we should nurture and maintain in our lives, but we also discover the characteristics of God.

Many religions and ideologies have rules and guidelines to follow but few that contain an invitation for us to participate in an intimate relationship with the Holy God of the universe. There are many religions with many religious leaders but only One who died for humankind and only One who conquered death.

Throughout the pages of Scripture, we see God as a relational person. In Genesis, He walked with Adam and Eve in the garden. Abraham was called a "friend of God." In the New Testament the church is referred to as the "bride of Christ" in a picture of the most intimate of relationships. When Christ walked the earth, He continually invested time and energy in relationships. The Gospels record that Jesus "had compassion on them"; He healed their sicknesses, fed them when they were hungry, and raised their dead.

Jesus desired much more than just a casual contact with humankind. Note the following miracle recorded in the book of Mark:

A large crowd followed and pressed around him. And a woman was there who had been subject to bleeding for twelve years. She had suffered a great deal under the care of many doctors and had spent all she had, yet instead of getting better she grew worse. When she heard about Jesus, she came up behind him in the crowd and touched his cloak, because she thought, "If I just touch his clothes, I will be healed." Immediately her bleeding stopped and she felt in her body that she was freed from her suffering.

At once Jesus realized that power had gone out from him. He turned around in the crowd and asked, "Who touched my clothes?" "You see the people crowding against you," his disciples answered, "and yet you can ask, 'Who touched me?'" But Jesus kept looking around to see who had done it. Then the woman, knowing what had happened to her, came and fell at his feet and, trembling with fear, told him the whole truth. He said to her, "Daughter, your faith has healed you. Go in peace and be freed from your suffering." (5:24–34)

This miracle is recorded in three of the four Gospels. This woman had a severe medical issue. She had done all she could do to try to repair the problem on her own, but nothing she had done worked for her. She was desperate to be healed. She didn't want a relationship with Jesus; she didn't want to deter Him from His agenda or distract Him from what He was doing, but she did want to be healed. She believed she could touch His garment, be healed, and leave unnoticed. Jesus was not going to let her get away with that. His disciples were perplexed because many people crowded around Jesus; many people were likely touching Him. Jesus was looking for someone in particular. Finally, the woman fell at His feet and confessed, allowing Jesus to make a relational connection.

In the miracle of this healing, Jesus could have just let her go; she had exercised her faith and had received what she longed for. Jesus was on His way to heal the daughter of one of the synagogue rulers. It was an important mission for an important person. But amid the crowds and the pressure, Jesus stopped to make a relational connection with this woman. His actions created a longer lasting impact on her life than just her healing. Jesus left a legacy mark on her life. Certainly, He wanted her to be healed, but Jesus also wanted her to "go in peace" and to be "freed from suffering." She came in hope and fear, but she left both healed and encouraged. She left with an understanding of Jesus that was more than just seeing Him as her Healer. He was her source of peace, and He was her Savior from suffering.

I have pondered this passage for a long time, and it has helped change my perspective on other Scriptures and my perspective on life. In the early years of my relationship with my beautiful wife, she lovingly referred to me as "socially handicapped." It was (and still is to some extent) an accurate description of my personality. Social interactions don't come naturally to me. I am one of those people who tend to be uncomfortable in a crowd and nervous at social gatherings. I have grown in this area but still struggle with it.

Early in my relationship with God, I viewed Him as my boss and viewed myself as His employee. He gave me rules to follow, and I did my best to follow them. My behavior was based on my need of Him alone. Much like the woman who suffered this ailment in the Bible, I wanted to see God, touch His garment, get my ticket into heaven, and move on with my life.

I was completely sincere but totally ignorant of what God really wanted from me. I knew I really didn't have anything to offer God so I committed to follow orders, report in when necessary, and maintain a professional Christian character. I became a classic twentieth-century Pharisee.

I had the best of intentions but couldn't see that God desires more. He is not satisfied with my knowing Him only as an authority figure. He wants me to know Him as Lord *and* Savior *and* Father. He wants me to obey the rules but not just because I am morally obligated to or because I am afraid of the consequences. He wants me to obey because of my great love for Him. He desires a relationship with me, and He desires that I know Him more.

He desires the same of you.

He has given you a foundational principle to live by, and He wants you to understand it. He has a purpose for your life, and He wants you to fulfill it. He wants to reveal Himself to you as more than just the Creator of life.

He wants a relationship.

In Matthew 15:8–9, Jesus quotes a passage from Isaiah: "These people honor me with their lips, but their hearts are far from me. They worship me in vain; their teachings are but rules taught by men."

The Pharisees that Christ was referring to in this passage didn't get it. They were focused solely on the rules of Scripture and their religious tradition. They missed the once-in-a-lifetime chance to have a relationship with the Messiah they had been seeking. We often look at the Pharisees with contempt for their religious philosophies but fail to examine our own beliefs with the same scrutiny. For a long time I was a modern-day Pharisee. I was an exceptional student in Bible class. I went to church every Sunday. I prayed at mealtime and judged others for not being as religious as I was. The parallels are astounding, yet I was totally blind to them.

When I was twenty-six years old, I had a real encounter with God. I was on a business trip in Ohio. I remember being totally dissatisfied with trying to follow the rules and coming up short on joy. That night I cried out to God. I asked Him who He really was. God spoke to me in a way that is completely indescribable. I felt His presence in that room. I worshipped Him for the first time, and that night He changed my life forever. I still had nothing worth giving Him, but I totally surrendered everything I had anyway. Then I began to understand God as more than the image I had created in my head. Then I met the real Jesus Christ and started a true relationship with God. Then God insisted on making that relational connection with me.

Since that night I have had to rewire some of my thought processes. I still struggle with my old way of thinking sometimes. I tend to take a "bank account" approach to relationships. As long as I have invested in others by helping them out or providing for a need, I then feel like I can withdraw some from that account and ask them for help. The issue with that thought process is that God gave everything to me, and I cannot repay His magnitude of grace. God is making a relational connection without any strings attached.

He desires to make and keep a relational connection with you. To facilitate that relational connection, God provides the Bible as a means of revealing His character. He provides the Holy Spirit to dwell within us, and He provides a history of actions and influences that help us learn more about Him.

The greatest act of love and grace God performed in human history is the brutal beating and death of Jesus on the cross. But in His death, just as in His life, Jesus was making a relational connection. Romans 5:8 is a familiar passage of Scripture: "But God demonstrates his own love for us in this: While we were still sinners, Christ died for us."

Even before the creation of the world, God knew humankind would reject Him. God alone is responsible for setting the price of redemption. He could have required something else; He could have required something less. It was entirely His decision. In His wisdom almighty God set the price of man's redemption to be the blood of Jesus. Why? Because of love. God set His heart on man; he chose to. He developed an entire plan including the sacrifice required for the sole purpose of demonstrating His love for us. The depth of His love for us and His desire for a close relationship with us is immeasurable.

In His three-year ministry on earth, Jesus had different circles of influence with people, and He was intentional about the time He spent investing in others. Jesus healed, fed, and helped large groups of people. Many of those people knew about Jesus but stopped short of a relationship with Him when it became inconvenient or difficult. Amid all of His followers, Jesus had a profound impact on twelve distinct men we know today as His disciples. These twelve men were loyal followers who changed their direction in life in order to learn from Him. Among the twelve disciples the Gospels list three men—Peter, James, and John—who were His closest confidants. These three men had their lives radically impacted, and each of them played a crucial role in the growth of the church and the spread of the gospel. At the end of His life on earth, only one of His disciples, John, remained loyal enough to follow Jesus to the cross. Although not any more or less important than any of the other disciples, John stayed with Jesus to the end because of the close relationship they shared.

Your circle of influence likely mirrors that of Jesus. You likely have one or two people in your life you are extremely close to. Outside your inner circle of friends or family is a larger circle of people you would consider great friends but not best friends. Beyond those people are additional levels. With each person you interact with, you have some level of influence. The influence is there, but only you can determine the impact. You determine the strength of the relational connection.

Relationship is the key to discipleship. Jesus chose twelve men with whom He invested His time. At the end of His ministry, he left them with the command to go make other disciples. He could have waited until the technology was available to spread the gospel message over the radio waves, but instead He chose to pour into the lives of twelve men so they would pour into others' lives. That command is relevant to us as well.

You impact the lives of those around you every day. Consciously or unconsciously you are making a relational connection with the people you encounter. Just as God chose the type of relational connection He makes with us, so we also must choose the type of relational connections we make with Him and with other people. God's desire is to have a radical impact on our lives. Our desire should also be to have a radical impact on others.

Relationships are a key part of our lives. The right relationship with God is the only way to realize fully your potential in life and the best way to have a positive impact on others' lives. God's plan includes the indwelling of the Holy Spirit in the life of a believer and the opportunity for you to listen for God's direction in your life without a translator or a rule book. It is like being in a foreign country and having a personal tour guide instead of just a map.

A relational connection with God built on the foundational principle of Scripture changes lives regardless of race, religion, or social status. Throughout history there have been countless examples of people who have been forever impacted and altered by a realization of God's character and love.

In 620 BC, King Josiah realized the holiness of God after he heard the words of Scripture in the temple at Jerusalem. This new understanding changed his life and spared the nation from imminent judgment (2 Kings 22:1–20). Two hundred years later the nation of Israel experienced another radical change after hearing the words of Scripture when they returned to rebuild Jerusalem under Nehemiah's leadership (Neh. 8:18–9:3).

Shortly after the death and resurrection of Jesus, a Pharisee famous for persecuting Christians had an encounter with God that changed his life forever (Acts 9:1–22). After this event Paul spent years reexamining what he knew about the Bible and discovered a relationship with Jesus Christ as Savior that he never knew before.

Fast-forward to the present time. God is still making relational connections that have life-changing impacts. I have personally witnessed the power of a relationship with God based on Scripture in my own life and in the lives of some of my family and friends.

God wants an intimate relationship with you. He can impact your life and show you how to fulfill your purpose. He wants you to understand and respond to Him. He wants you to have a changed life, a better life, a meaningful life.

If you don't have a real relationship with God, you don't get it. If you attend church but have no joy, you don't get it. If you stand in church but do not sing His praises, you don't get it. If you have read parts of the Bible but have never heard Him speak to you, then you don't get it. The Pharisees didn't get it. The unnamed woman in the Bible who was healed got it. Do you get it?

Dan's Story

Dan was at a crossroad. He knew there was much more to God and the Bible than what he believed when he was young. He had taken some hard roads and, at one point or another, abandoned most of the moral code he once believed reigned supreme. As he searched for answers to the meaning of life, Dan came to a point one night where his mind and heart were restless. He couldn't focus on anything else and cried out in anguish. He verbally asked God the question, "Who are you?"

Suddenly years of Bible stories and verses came to mind but in a much different context. It wasn't just a list of rules and stories reflecting what to do and not do. It was a picture of God. The realization brought him to his knees. All this time Dan's understanding of God was wrong. God wasn't just the keeper of heaven and the judge of man. Instead, He was someone more. Someone real. It was like God came down and filled the room with a presence so strong it made Dan tremble inside. Suddenly, God wasn't some distant being; He was a close God. He was a God who wanted Dan. Not what Dan could do but Dan the person.

That night Dan had to start over. He suddenly had a much better understanding of who Jesus is and a deeper reverence for God. Dan begged Jesus to save him from the eternal punishment of his sins and to be the Lord of his life.

Dan began to study the Bible as a great biography of God. The moral code was still there, but he chose to follow it motivated by love instead of obligation. It was much easier that way, almost natural. This was a new road for Dan, an exciting one. His experience with God that night and his commitment to study and learn more were key factors in preparing Dan for the change in position that was coming next.

Chapter

6

DENYING A BIBLICAL PRINCIPLE

Are the power of a scriptural principle and an intimate relationship with Jesus really a big deal? We have looked at some of the Scripture references that promise blessings and peace for those who seek God, but is there another side to the coin? If seeking God through the Bible brings joy in our lives, does ignoring it bring unpleasant consequences? History and the declarations of Scripture provide the answer to that question.

The Bible gives us many examples in the Old Testament of times when the nation of Israel ignored God's word and realized some severe consequences for their apathy toward God. Isaiah 6 records one of God's judgments on His people:

> He said, "Go and tell this people: "'Be ever hearing, but never understanding; be ever seeing, but never perceiving.' Make the heart of this people calloused; make their ears dull and close their eyes. Otherwise they might see with their eyes, hear with their ears, understand with their hearts, and turn and be healed." Then I said, "For how long, O Lord?" And he answered: "Until the cities lie ruined and without inhabitant, until the houses are left deserted and the fields ruined and ravaged, until the LORD has sent everyone far away and the land is utterly forsaken. And though a tenth remains in the land, it will again be laid waste." (vv. 9–13)

This is a harsh passage. According to the first verse, Isaiah received this vision in the year King Uzziah died. King Uzziah reigned in Jerusalem for fifty-two years, and before him his father reigned for twenty-nine years. The book of 2 Kings states that both of these kings did

DENYING A BIBLICAL PRINCIPLE

what was right in the eyes of God, but both of them refused to tear down the "high places." These "high places" were hilltop pagan worship centers the Israelites inherited from their conquest of the Canaanites. The use of these worship centers was forbidden in Scripture, but the Israelites continued to use them. In addition to having a combined eighty-one years of freedom to do the right thing under the leadership of these kings, the people also had the prophets Amos and Hosea condemning their sin and their spiritual adultery against God. With the solid preaching of these prophets and the freedom to follow God's decrees, the people chose to ignore His word, thereby forfeiting divine protection, and they brought about the fulfillment of Isaiah's prophecy.[3]

The nation of Israel is not alone in the cultural drift to ignore God's principle. In our current culture we also have the freedom to do the right thing and the encouragement of solid men of God to heed the word of the Lord; yet, too often, we fall into the same pattern that drove Israel to judgment. Many modern-day pastors and teachers warn of impending judgment against wicked cultures. Romans 1, beginning in verse 18, records the degradation of all human existence for those who choose not to seek God as the answer to their quest for purpose.

The wrath of God is being revealed from heaven against all the godlessness and wickedness of men who suppress the truth by their wickedness, since what may be known about God is plain to them, because God has made it plain to them. For since the creation of the world God's invisible qualities—his eternal power and divine nature—have been clearly seen, being understood from what has been made, so that men are without excuse.

For although they knew God, they neither glorified him as God nor gave thanks to him, but their thinking became futile and their foolish hearts were darkened. Although they claimed to be wise, they became fools and exchanged the glory of the immortal God for images made to look like mortal man and birds and animals and reptiles.

Therefore God gave them over in the sinful desires of their hearts to sexual impurity for the degrading of their bodies with one another. They exchanged the truth of God for a lie, and worshiped and served created things rather than the Creator—who is forever praised. Amen.

Because of this, God gave them over to shameful lusts. Even their women exchanged natural relations for unnatural ones. In the same way the men also abandoned natural relations with women and were inflamed with lust for one another. Men committed indecent acts with other men, and received in themselves the due penalty for their perversion.

Furthermore, since they did not think it worthwhile to retain the knowledge of God, he gave them over to a depraved mind, to do what ought not to be done. They have become filled with every kind of wickedness, evil, greed and depravity. They are full of envy, murder, strife, deceit and malice. They are gossips, slanderers, God-haters, insolent, arrogant and boastful; they invent ways of doing evil; they disobey their parents; they are senseless, faithless, heartless, ruthless. (Rom. 1:18–31)

Following the progression in this passage:

1. God has made Himself known through creation; His invisible qualities are apparent enough in the world to spur man to seek Him further. God's character is revealed through creation, man's conscience, and the Scriptures.

2. Mankind chose not to glorify Him or give thanks to Him but instead chose to make material idols for worship. This has been the pattern of many civilizations throughout the ages. In ancient times those idols tended to be wood carvings or cast images; in today's society the idols take on much more complex forms of overindulgences in entertainment, material possessions, careers, or addictions.

3. The next step in the depravity progression is that humankind continued to indulge deeper in sinful desires. In other words, sin breeds more sin.

4. Then the sinful desires lead them to shameful lusts. A quick look at modern advertising campaigns and the dominance of homosexual agendas in the media is enough evidence to support that our society is heading down that road.

According to the 2010 U.S. Census Bureau and several established national surveys, homosexual couples constitute less than 3 percent of American households; yet most television shows and movies depict homosexuals in some context as a common and normal lifestyle. Do you ever wonder why that is? The gay marriage debate is one of the top political issues of our time.

Secular society has communicated that calling homo-sexuality a sin is hate speech and considered an attack on tolerance. Ultimately this is not a tolerance issue, nor is it an issue of condemnation; it is a discernment issue. If the Bible is our foundational principle and the Bible calls homosexuality sin, then it must be what the Bible says it is. Referencing this passage, the more we ignore God, the greater the proliferation of homosexuality, sexual immorality, and evil will be in our society.

Finally, at the end of the chapter, God gives them over to complete depravity of the mind. This progression of depravity results in a person whose character is altogether vile. The list of character traits at the end of this passage is considered wicked even by secular standards. According to the last verse in this chapter, this level of depravity comes not out of ignorance but instead out of rebellion against God. It is a choice. The choice belongs to us as a culture, and the choice belongs to you as an individual.

The fate of those who completely ignore God's directive on life is harsh. The Bible describes it as a hopeless existence. It may not seem so bad for a while, but just like unhealthy eating or lack of exercise, eventually it will catch up to you.

In between those who deny God and those who embrace Him are those who play the religion game. In general these "good" people go to church and live by a moral standard but have no focus on the Bible as their principle, nor do they have any tangible fruit in their lives.

According to recent polls, 75 to 85 percent of Americans claim to be Christian.[4] Statistically that is a large number. That number is also in stark contrast to what the Bible says: "Enter through the narrow gate. For wide is the gate and broad is the road that leads to destruction, and many enter through it. But small is the gate and narrow the road that leads to life, and only a few find it" (Matt. 7:13–14).

If these verses are accurate, then there must be more to life than the average American Christian is living. Average American Christians are easy to spot. They go to church but do not worship. They may know the books of the Bible but do not study it. They recite a blessing before dinner but otherwise rarely pray. The average American Christian has religion, moral ethics, and maybe even some semblance of a church attendance record, but does not have a relationship with God. The relationship piece is a choice just as spiritual growth is a choice. These choices require work.

The call of God is a call to an active relationship, not to passive religion. As I look at Jesus' miracles in the Gospels, more than half of them required some form of action on the part of the person for whom the miracle is intended. Jesus did not need them to participate in order to perform the miracle, but in many cases He did ask them to do something. Sometimes it was as simple as "go wash in the Pool of Siloam" or "go show yourself to the priest" or "fill the jars with water" or "put out into deep water and let down the nets for a catch." No matter what the task was, it required some level of actionable involvement.

In 2 Kings 5, a man named Naaman sought the prophet Elisha to be healed of his leprosy. Elisha told him to go wash seven times in the Jordan. Naaman was so offended by this silly request that he almost went back home with his leprosy untouched. Fortunately, his servants convinced him to try it and he did; the result was that Naaman was healed. Could God have healed Naaman without his taking this action step? Yes, but it wasn't about the healing as much as it was about the lesson of faith.

God is calling us to action today. That call is not just a regular church attendance and a moral life. It is more. It is a call to remain in Christ and bear fruit. "No branch can bear fruit by itself; it must remain in the vine. Neither can you bear fruit unless you remain in me. I am the vine; you are the branches. If a man remains in me and I in him, he will bear much fruit;

apart from me, you can do nothing. If anyone does not remain in me, he is like a branch that is thrown away and withers; such branches are picked up, thrown into the fire and burned" (John 15:4–6).

We do not control the fruit we bear; it is an evidence of what we do. We *do* control how much we remain in Him. We control how much we study His word. We control how much we obey His word. We control how much, if any, we worship Him. We control how much we show love to others. We control how we prioritize our lives.

There is no neutral position here. We need to take responsibility for our own decisions; we are either choosing to seek God, or we are drifting from Him. Choosing to seek is an intentional action that must be maintained. Anyone who chooses not to seek God drifts away from Him and closer to wickedness. If you imagine this as a car on a hill, it is intentional for the driver to engage the clutch and press on the gas pedal. Without this intentional action, the car rolls downhill. In Jesus' own words: "He who is not with me is against me, and he who does not gather with me, scatters" (Luke 11:23).

In nature nothing improves by being stagnant. Animals that do not hunt for food die of starvation. A tree planted in a bucket will eventually die because it cannot grow its roots beyond the confines of the container. Growth and improvement are part of the natural process. Growth can also be painful. Anyone who has ever visited a gym or enlisted in a fitness program can support the claim that building muscle and improving body tone are painful.

Mental and spiritual growth also requires effort. Seeking after God requires effort. Following the commands and guidelines of Scripture takes effort, but the Bible and the testimony of those who seek to obey God prove that such efforts are beneficial. "The man who says, 'I know him,' but does not do what he commands is a liar, and the truth is not in him. But if anyone obeys his word, God's love is truly made complete in him. This is how we know we are in him: Whoever claims to live in him must walk as Jesus did" (1 John 2:4–6).

The risk we take is with our own eternal destiny. Our response to the Bible as the defining principle in our lives is characterized by Jesus in the parable of the sower in Matthew 13. Some will hear but not take enough interest to dig deeper and choose not to make the effort to seek God. For them Jesus says the evil one will snatch the word away. Others will hear it and take it to heart but will not remain faithful in their quest. Their spiritual growth will have no root, and they will not last. Their spiritual zeal will be short-lived and they will soon fall back into their routine. Still others will hear it but will lose focus and get distracted by the worries of the world and the deceitfulness of wealth. Only the last soil described as the good soil will hear the word and seek to understand with lifelong consistency. Those believers persevere and seek to develop a deeper understanding of God's Word. They will also energize and encourage others to seek after God and to discover their purpose. Those are the true Christians who will leave a legacy of godly character.

Paul wrote his letter to the Philippians while imprisoned in Rome. In his letter Paul shares his desire to continue to grow: "I want to know Christ and the power of his resurrection and the fellowship of sharing in his sufferings, becoming like him in his death, and so, somehow, to attain to the resurrection from the dead" (Phil. 3:10–11).

Paul knew that growing was a choice, and he knew that choice would not be easy. Nevertheless, Paul counted it a privilege to suffer for the sake of Christ. The current church culture does not know much of suffering the way the early church encountered it. Still, for those who seek God, the road is not easy. It should not be easy. If it is easy for you, it may not be real.

The journey is not easy but it is rewarding. Ultimately it is a decision of priority that requires continual focus.

Similar to exercise, the more you choose to do it, the healthier you become and the easier it gets. The more you choose not to exercise, the unhealthier your body gets, and the more difficult it becomes to start exercising again.

In Ephesians 6, Paul describes the life of a believer with the analogy of a battlefield. In 1 Corinthians 9, Paul correlates the life of a believer to a race. Both of these analogies indicate that living with the Bible as your foundational principle and seeking after God to fulfill your purpose requires both training and perseverance. The reward is also clear: it is the reward of victory, and it is a reward of legacy. It is a reward of life.

Dan's Story

Paul went to a Christian high school just like Dan, but after graduation Paul quickly dropped his moral standard in exchange for several of life's most enticing addictions. Paul is now divorced, in debt, and bearing through each day of a job he doesn't like.

Then there is Mary. Mary never did pretend to be a Christian. She fell madly in love and married a man who had enough money to take care of her the rest of her life. Some people say she has it all. She drives a nice car and wears the latest fashion, but deep in her heart she suffers. She covers her misery with makeup and a smile, but she lacks the confidence of someone who knows true love.

If you asked Dan about his relationship with God, he would probably tell you he didn't consider himself a true believer before the night God rattled his heart. Dan saw all too clearly the fate of others who also called themselves Christians but ultimately walked away from the real God of the Bible.

Dan sometimes wondered why his life didn't turn out like Paul's or Mary's. He knew it well could have. He had been in a place in his life where he abandoned his moral code. He had also known the hollowness of chasing stuff that only brought pleasure for a short time. His heart breaks for them. Their story isn't unique. There are so many just like them, people who "grin and bear it." They sometimes seek refuge in self-help books and magazines. They sometimes consume themselves in a project or with a collection. They carry their emotional baggage and indulge in whatever temporarily kills the pain. This isn't how life is supposed to be.

Chapter 7

POSITION

Generally, when we take family road trips, my wife does most of the driving. While both of us are good drivers, my preference is to navigate. I enjoy the confidence of knowing where we are, where we are going, and how to get there. I believe most people, myself included, don't enjoy the feeling of being lost; it makes us feel powerless and sometimes afraid. We are much more comfortable in familiar territories and with our daily routines, but there is still great value in stopping to look around and see where we are.

Position defines where we are, but it is not limited to geographical location; it is tied to our position in time, space, and state of being. Position can also be used to describe where we are in relation to God.

For example, if you assume that career success is the pinnacle of your life, then your physical position will be consumed with work. Your mental position will be focused on climbing the corporate ladder. Your relational position with your family may suffer as you drive your career success at the expense of everything else. You will become known primarily for your profession. You could become a great doctor or businessman and be recognized and remembered only as Dr. Evans or Mr. Smith, the executive, but does that provide fulfillment in life?

Our current society is plagued with depression and thoughts of self-worthlessness in part because of what we are being taught about our position. The modern-day educational system and media send a unified message that humans evolved from apes, that the creation of the world was an accident, and that the planet is headed for imminent destruction. Combine all of those messages with the societal desensitizing of the population by means of graphic violence and sexual enticement, and the result is a society that is demoralized and depressed.

If I believe my position is that I am an evolved animal living on an accidental rock in space doomed for destruction, then my natural inclination is going to be apathy and inadequacy. What should I do in life? Does anything I do matter? Do I matter? This line of thinking leads to a hopeless belief in life, and yet this is the message of our teachers and culture. If my position is truly meaningless and if nothing I do will ultimately matter in the grand scheme of history, then my goal will likely become self-satisfaction. The means of that self-satisfaction can come in a variety of short-lived indulgences. Indulgences can take the form of the excitement of travel, a favorite television show, or an obsession with a sports team. Like many of life's pleasures, travel and entertainment are not bad if they are kept in moderation. The danger is when these enjoyments become an integral part of our existence. Indulgences could also be something a bit more addictive like alcohol, drugs, or infidelity.

To help us combat the resulting feeling of senselessness that comes from believing what we are told about our position, a myriad of self-help books and programs are designed to help us feel good about ourselves. Unfortunately most of these materials lack the ability to help us fully understand and internalize our position. We are bombarded with false messages of self-hope. Although the wording may vary, the message is something like this: "If you believe in yourself, you can do anything." If I believe strongly enough, does it make my belief real? How many people audition to be the next great singer or dancer on any given reality television show? Yet only one can win, and most everyone else goes home with shattered dreams. On average a single state lottery each week has one winner and eighteen million losers, but every one of them had enough belief to purchase a ticket. The message sounds good, but too often it is just a marketing tactic that someone is using for their own profit; in real life it's rarely true. The understanding of who we really are must come from something other than a strong belief in ourselves.

The question then becomes: Is the modern cultural definition of position true? This is where foundational principle ties in. If your principle follows the modern-day scientific approach or commonly accepted social beliefs, then yes, we are only evolved beings. We are here by accident, and we are doomed to destruction. Following that thought to its logical conclusion means the purpose of man—both collectively and individually—is to save the planet, ensure the proliferation of our species, and live life to indulge our pleasures to the best of our capabilities. There really isn't much else to look forward to. Even meager attempts to help others in need or perform good deeds has no real lasting effect as those you help will ultimately suffer the same fate as you. They, too, will one day be gone, and a few years from now that good deed will be gone and forgotten.

This thought process seems depressing, but I cannot follow the common world principle to any other conclusion. It doesn't yield anything but a meaningless existence.

Where are you? It is a good question.

I have always been fascinated in studying the questions God asks. This is one of the many traits that distinguish God's character from man's character. When a person asks a question, it is in the pursuit of an answer; when God asks a question, it is often meant to stir thought. By design it is how our brains work. From the dreaded high school final exam to simply asking the person next to you for the time, questions stir thought processes.

This all ties back to position in the question, Where are you? It is the first question asked by God recorded in Scripture. It is found in Genesis 3:9. In the context of this Scripture, Adam and Eve had just disobeyed God by eating the fruit of the tree of the knowledge of good and evil from which they were forbidden to eat. Having disobeyed God, they realized they were naked and hid from God in the garden. God knew what they had done and where they were. He knew everything happening in that moment and everything that would happen as a result of that moment even before they were created. Still, He asked the question, "Where are you?" Interestingly enough, Adam never really answered God's question. As God probed deeper with Adam, he finally admitted that he had eaten from the tree. Adam made sure Eve shared in the guilt and punishment due them, and they were both expelled from the garden of Eden forever.

There are several dimensions to position. The first is physical location; I am at my desk, in my house, in the city of Albany, in the state of Georgia. As important as this information can be, position must be examined in more than just the physical location dimension. You already know where you are physically, just as God already knew where Adam and Eve were.

God was not looking for Adam to recite his physical location; His intent was to stir Adam to think deeper and connect on a relational level. Where was he spiritually, intellectually, emotionally? It is a question of condition. Adam, now a sinner, was in a much different position relationally than before his act of disobedience. Prior to his rebellion Adam walked with God in the garden. God lovingly gave him everything he needed. He provided a paradise residence, a helpmate from his own flesh, and a purpose in being the sole steward of the garden of Eden. This burden-free existence and fellowship with God had been broken. Adam's new position was that of independence from God and a pursuit of something beyond what God had intended for him. Unfortunately Adam failed to understand his position and started the world's first blame game, throwing his responsibility to Eve, who then passed it on to the serpent.

Being constantly aware of your physical and relational position can be a great deterrent to potential sin. Reference 2 Samuel 11:1–2: "In the spring, at the time when kings go off to war, David sent Joab out with the king's men and the whole Israelite army. . . . One evening David got up from his bed and walked around on the roof of the palace. From the roof he saw a woman bathing."

The rest of the story is well-known history. David committed adultery with Uriah's wife, tried to cover it up, and then orchestrated the man's murder. Though this one sin is the most famous tarnish on David's reputation, the Bible says he was a "man after God's heart." David was a great king and a committed follower of God. He was a strong leader and a devout psalmist. He was a man of deep prayer and of great faith in God. First Kings 15:5 says, "David had done what was right in the eyes of the LORD and had not failed to keep any of the LORD's commandments all the days of his life—except in the case of Uriah the Hittite." David was not a bad guy or a bad king. In fact, he is revered as one of the greatest kings in all of Israel's history.

So how did a man like David, a man after God's own heart, fall prey to such temptation? His position had a significant influence on his decision. Note 2 Samuel 11:1–2 again: "In the spring, . . . when kings go off to war . . . David got up from his bed." David was king; he should have been out on the battlefield with Joab, not lying in his bed. For seventeen years prior to this event, David had enjoyed God's prosperity. Israel had won every military campaign; David's wealth had increased, and his popularity with the people was at its peak. In times of prosperity, our hearts can turn from a desperate need of God to a more casual relationship or, even worse, the neglect of a relationship with God.

David was in the wrong place at the wrong time. Not just physically, although that played a part in his ultimate blunder, but David was in the wrong place spiritually. If he had been in the right place spiritually, he likely would have been in the right place physically as well and could have potentially avoided one of the biggest mistakes of his life.

The Bible also lists examples of people who were in the right position when God called. Notably all of these references are men with a reputation of having a strong relationship with God.

"Some time later God tested Abraham. He said to him, 'Abraham!' 'Here I am,' he replied" (Gen. 22:1). At the end of Genesis 21, the Bible says Abraham planted a tamarisk tree as a marker of a place of worship and he called on the name of the Lord there. Abraham was in the right position physically and spiritually to hear God and to respond correctly.

"And God spoke to Israel in a vision at night and said, 'Jacob! Jacob!' 'Here I am,' he replied" (Gen. 46:2). Prior to this verse, the Bible says that Jacob "set out with all that was his, and when he reached Beersheba, he offered sacrifices to the God of his father Isaac" (Gen. 46:1). Jacob was a crafty man, but during this time in his life, he was in the right position to hear God and to respond.

"When the LORD saw that he had gone over to look, God called to him from within the bush, 'Moses! Moses!' And Moses said, 'Here I am'" (Exod. 3:4). Prior to this encounter, Moses was tending the flock of his father-in-law and led the flock to the far side of the desert toward Horeb, the mountain of God. Moses grew up a prince of Egypt but was exiled and spent forty years in humble circumstances to get a better understanding of his position.

"Then the LORD called Samuel. Samuel answered, 'Here I am'" (1 Sam. 3:4). In 1 Samuel 3:1, "The boy . . . ministered before the LORD under Eli." Samuel was an answer to prayer for his barren mother, Hannah. He was dedicated to God at an early age and was keenly aware of his position even as a young boy.

"In Damascus there was a disciple named Ananias. The Lord called to him in a vision, 'Ananias!' 'Yes, Lord,' he answered" (Acts 9:10). Ananias was a disciple of Christ and one of the leaders in the Damascus church. Earlier in Acts 9, Saul requested letters from the high priests giving him authority to arrest any follower of Jesus in Damascus. After God calls Ananias in verse 10, He instructed him to go find Saul and heal his blindness. After some level of hesitation, Ananias obeyed. His act of obedience marked the beginning of Paul's ministry to the Gentiles.

In the case of each of these men, God called them first before He gave them direction. Notice the difference between the reaction of these men and Adam's response: "I heard you in the garden, and I was afraid because I was naked; so I hid" (Gen. 3:10). Adam responded by telling God what he heard, what he felt, what he knew, and what he did, but he never answered the question God was asking.

Isaiah was one of the greatest prophets of the Old Testament. His vision is recorded in chapter 6. In his vision Isaiah saw God seated on the throne of heaven high and exalted. This vision was clear and powerful. It reminded Isaiah of his position relative to a holy God. Isaiah responds in a penitent manner: "'Woe to me!' I cried. 'I am ruined! For I am a man of unclean lips, and I live among a people of unclean lips, and my eyes have seen the King, the LORD Almighty'" (Isa. 6:5).

After his humble confession, Isaiah is told that his sins are atoned for and that his guilt is taken away. The next statement is a question from God, "Whom shall I send?"

Isaiah's response: "Here am I. Send me!"

Isaiah knew where he was spiritually at the beginning of his vision. He knew he had to be cleansed. Only then could he offer himself to God's service. God used Isaiah because he had a correct perspective on his position.

In the New Testament the parable of the prodigal son illustrates the grace and compassion of our Lord and our need for repentance. The parable also tells us something about position:

Jesus continued: "There was a man who had two sons. The younger one said to his father, 'Father, give me my share of the estate.' So he divided his property between them.

"Not long after that, the younger son got together all he had, set off for a distant country and there squandered his wealth in wild living. After he had spent everything, there was a severe famine in that whole country, and he began to be in need. So he went and hired himself out to a citizen of that country, who sent him to his fields to feed pigs. He longed to fill his stomach with the pods that the pigs were eating, but no one gave him anything.

"When he came to his senses, he said, 'How many of my father's hired men have food to spare, and here I am starving to death! I will set out and go back to my father and say to him: Father, I have sinned against heaven and against you.'" (Luke 15:11–18)

The central theme of the parable is the father's acceptance of the son when he returns. It parallels God the Father and His longing for us to come to Him. There is also an aspect of the son's thought process in verse 17 worth noting. "When he came to his senses," he realized where he was. Not only did he realize where he was but where he had been and where he could be. His position is both of physical desperation and of relational need. He is willing to change both for the better. He is willing to move back home and willing to accept a much different relationship with his father. Once he realizes his position, he takes immediate action to change it.

The question for you is this: Do you realize your position? If so, are you willing to change it if necessary? Do you know where you are, where you have been, and where you could be?

In Luke 7, Jesus is confronted with a man who needs help. The man is not named in Scripture, but we know that he was a professional officer in the Roman army. This officer had a servant who was deathly ill. Apparently the officer placed a high value on his servant so he asked Jesus to come and heal him. While Jesus was on the way to his house, the Roman officer sent friends to Jesus with the following message: "Lord, don't trouble yourself, for I do not deserve to have you come under my roof. That is why I did not even consider myself worthy to come to you. But say the word, and my servant will be healed. For I myself am a man under authority, with soldiers under me. I tell this one, 'Go,' and he goes; and that one, 'Come,' and he comes.

I say to my servant, 'Do this,' and he does it" (Luke 7:6–8).

The next verse records Christ's response: "When Jesus heard this, he was amazed at him, and turning to the crowd following him, he said, 'I tell you, I have not found such great faith even in Israel'" (Luke 7:9).

Jesus was amazed at this Roman army officer because he understood his position. More important, this man understood his position relative to Jesus. For His entire life Jesus was surrounded by people who knew enough about the Messianic prophecies to recognize His position, but most of them failed to do so. In contrast, the Roman officer, though he may not have fully understood who Jesus was, recognized his own unworthiness and understood the authority of Christ.

Do you understand your position enough to affect your faith? Do you understand what the Bible says about where you are?

Scripture is clear on the base position of a person. First and foremost, you are either lost or saved. The words "lost" and "saved" are common church words we use in our language. The more refined descriptions of these two opposing positions are "void of a true relationship with God" or "in a true relationship with God." At the end of all time, life comes down to one of these two positions. Matthew 25:31–33 says: "When the Son of Man comes in his glory, and all the angels with him, he will sit on his throne in heavenly glory. All the nations will be gathered before him, and he will separate the people one from one another as the shepherd separates the sheep from the goats. He will put the sheep on His right and the goats on the left."

There is no other position; you are either a saved sheep living in the grace and mercy of God, or you are a lost goat void of a relationship with God. For many that fact is not easy to accept. Logically we must fall back on foundational principle. Do you believe the Bible is absolute truth? If so, do you know enough about it to know what it says about your position? It is not a study to be taken lightly. Scripture paints a clear picture of us as wretched sinners, helpless and in desperate need of a Savior: "There is no one righteous, not even one; there is no one who understands, no one who seeks God. All have turned away, they have together become worthless; there is no one who does good, not even one" (Rom. 3:10–12). "For all have sinned and fall short of the glory of God" (Rom. 3:23).

Our spiritual position is set at our birth. We are sinners by nature, condemned to be separated from God, lost and void of relationship. No matter how good we think we are or how good we try to be, we cannot change our position. Only God can change our position. "He saved us, not because of righteous things we had done, but because of his mercy. He saved us through the washing of rebirth and renewal by the Holy Spirit" (Titus 3:5). "But God demonstrates his own love for us in this: While we were still sinners, Christ died for us" (Rom. 5:8). "For the wages of sin is death, but the gift of God is eternal life in Christ Jesus our Lord" (Rom. 6:23).

Through Christ, God provides mercy and grace to change our position, and the Bible paints a much different picture of us after we have surrendered our lives to His lordship. It is a picture of adopted children, dearly loved. It is a relational position. "In love he predestined us to be adopted as his sons through Jesus Christ" (Eph. 1:4–5). "Put your trust in the light while you have it, so that you may become sons of light" (John 12:36).

The fact that we cannot change our own position does not alleviate us from the responsibility of our lives. The Bible clearly communicates our responsibility to believe and to seek God. "If you confess with your mouth, 'Jesus is Lord,' and believe in your heart that God raised him from the dead, you will be saved" (Rom. 10:9). "You will seek me and find me when you seek me with all your heart" (Jer. 29:13). "Everyone who calls on the name of the Lord will be saved" (Rom. 10:13).

These and many other Scripture passages communicate that we are accountable to seek. To seek God in knowledge and in relationship takes intentional effort but yields life-changing results.

Are you seeking God? What is your position? Knowing your position can and will change your life. Once you settle your relational position with God, you need to examine your other relational positions. Are you a husband or a wife? If you are, then are you acting in accordance with your foundational principle? Are you a father or mother? Are you an employee or employer? Each of these relational positions has some clear directives in the Bible. To follow these guidelines, we must know them, and to know them, we must seek them. Great relationships take effort, but great relationships often lead to great legacies.

What do you want your position to be? It is your responsibility in life to align your position with your foundational principle and to improve your life. It is your responsibility to seek to understand where you need to be and how to get there. You must be willing to accept your position and the consequences that relate to your position or to "come to your senses" and change your position. No one else can make the decision for you. Where are you?

Dan's Story

Before the night he encountered God, Dan had been through his fair share of dating relationships. No matter how hard he tried, each one failed miserably. He tried following all of the great advice he received from Hollywood movies. He began to believe he was destined to live his life alone. This thought made him sad and sometimes a bit resentful toward God.

Not long after Dan began his new relationship with Jesus, he met a beautiful girl at a friend's wedding. She was radiant and full of life. They began dating and were married a year later. The wedding was simple with a touch of elegance. Dan soon realized that he was responsible for taking care of someone other than himself. As this was new territory for Dan, he studied his principle to discover God's requirements of a husband. He felt like he should have already nailed this down, but his new wife was patient with him as he sorted out his life priorities based on his new position as husband and provider. He also studied his bride so that he could love her in the way that was uniquely suited to her personality. He felt that if God went to great extremes to show Dan what love really is, then Dan should do the same for his wife.

POSITION

Through his study of the Bible as his foundation, Dan also learned how to be a better father to their children, a better friend to others, and a better employee at work. Because of his solid foundation, Dan grew emotionally and spiritually stable. He found a great deal of satisfaction in his marriage, his family, and his job. Dan understood that a big part of his purpose in life was to be a godly husband, father, and friend, but in his heart Dan also longed to fulfill a greater purpose.

Chapter 1

PURPOSE

W hat is the purpose of man?" It is one of the great questions philosophers through the ages have asked. It is a question every person should resolve within themselves. Purpose is our reason for existence. Principle defines who we are, and position defines where we are, but purpose defines why we are. It is the way life is designed.

In looking at the world around us, everything that has a design has a purpose. Buildings, organizations, and tools all have a unique design to serve a unique purpose. Similarly, in nature, mountains, trees, and weather patterns all have a unique design for a unique purpose. Both physical and organizational structures have a purpose, and each individual component within the structure has a purpose. For example, a business not only has a purpose, but each individual within that business has a purpose. From the janitor who cleans the floors to the president of the company, each person has a unique and important function in making the business thrive. Each chapter in this book has a unique purpose that contributes to the purpose of the entire book.

Purpose fulfills the intent of the design. In business, marketing strategies are designed to satisfy a purpose to increase sales. In manufacturing, robotic equipment is designed to assemble parts. Golf courses are designed for recreation, and medicines are designed to heal.

Sometimes the purpose of something is not so obvious, but it is fallacy to assume it is void of purpose. In recent years the medical community has made some interesting discoveries about the human appendix, an organ that had previously been dismissed as useless. The appendix is now believed to play a vital role in the body's ability to prevent disease and to fight infection. Throughout history many human body parts were thought to be useless but later found to be vital to human development including the thyroid gland and the pituitary gland. The lack of an obvious or known purpose does not reflect a void of purpose.

Some things are created simply for the purpose of entertainment or enjoyment, while other items were created with a purpose for a time and are no longer required, like telephone booths or Civil War cannons.

The design and purpose concept thrives all around us both in what we create and in nature. Because it is so prevalent in our environment, each person must ask the question for themselves, "What is my purpose?" Viewing the concept of purpose through a defined principle and position can help provide the answer. Note this passage of Scripture from the book of Ephesians:

> Praise be to the God and Father of our Lord Jesus Christ, who has blessed us in the heavenly realms with every spiritual blessing in Christ. For he chose us in him before the creation of the world to be holy and blameless in his sight. In love he predestined us to be adopted as his sons through Jesus Christ, in accordance with his pleasure and will—to the praise of his glorious grace, which he has freely given us in the One he loves. (Eph. 1:3–6)

From this passage we know we were created to be holy and blameless in His sight. We are adopted as sons through Jesus for "the praise of his glorious grace" according to His will. Note that our position is to be holy and blameless adopted children. This position aligns our lives to fulfill the purpose of His glorification according to His pleasure and will. This chapter will take a closer look at what it means to be holy both individually and collectively.

The phrase "the praise of his glory" appears three times in Ephesians 1. During the English Reformation of the 1640s, the Westminster Catechism defined the chief end of man in the same manner: Man's chief end is to glorify God and to enjoy Him forever.

So then, how do we apply this? Purpose exists on two planes, collective and individual. Collectively all humankind has the same purpose: to glorify God. The collective glorification of God emanates from the acknowledgment that Jesus is Lord and Savior and the worship of Him alone. Scripture communicates that at the end of time, every man will confess that Jesus is Lord and will worship Him to the glory of God. "Therefore, God exalted him to the highest place and gave him the name that is above every name, that at the name of Jesus every knee should bow, in heaven and on earth and under the earth, and every tongue confess that Jesus Christ is Lord, to the glory of God the Father" (Phil. 2:9–11).

Just as individuals in a corporation may have different functions and different styles, each person contributes so the business can serve its purpose. God's design for the church follows the same pattern. The church is made of individuals with unique abilities and talents working together to collectively fulfill the purpose of the church to glorify God.

Micah 6:8 provides insight into what God requires of all humankind: "He has showed you, O man, what is good. And what does the LORD require of you? To act justly and to love mercy and to walk humbly with your God."

What is unique about these requirements is that they are a reflection of God's character. To exhibit these characteristics is a choice. If we don't focus on these requirements, then we will not be intentional about making the right decisions. Instead we will fall back into our natural state of being. By nature we are selfish, judgmental, and proud. In addition to our own natural inclinations, we are surrounded by the world's direction to be successful at any cost and to take credit for more than we deserve. Our natural characteristics and the messages of the world are in direct opposition to what God requires of us.

As a father, some of my most satisfying moments are when my girls follow my example in an act of kindness or love toward another person. At times my girls have seen me wash the dishes and clean the kitchen as an act of love and kindness toward my wife. There have also been times that I have watched them clean up each other's messes or clean up after their friends as an act of kindness. Moments like that warm my heart. It is a demonstration of the results I desire in my children. God has the same desire of us. When we choose to demonstrate characteristics that are holy, we are fulfilling our purpose by acting like we are made in the image of God. The last part of the verse also reinforces that we are to have a relationship with God, and that relationship is to be ongoing. It is a humble walk with God, not a standstill.

In the good and in the bad, children are often the greatest reflection of their parents. My wife and I reinforce this with our girls when they are going someplace without us. We ask them this question: "Whom do you represent?" The answer should always be: "I represent God and my family." We want our girls to understand that they represent God in what they do and that they also represent their mother and father. They know we expect them to represent us well. Why would this be any less of an expectation from God? This is why God calls us "adopted sons." We are His children and should be a reflection of His goodness. That is how we bring a smile to the face of a holy God. That is how we collectively glorify Him.

The second plane of purpose is individual purpose. Note in the Ephesians passage that our position and purpose are first and foremost to "*be* holy and blameless" and to "*be* adopted as sons." In the quest for purpose, we often confuse *being* with *doing*. Many ask, "What should I do to fulfill my purpose?" Although it is important to do the things that please God, the primary focus should be placed on "being" the right person, which results in "doing" the right things. Galatians 5 lists the fruit of the spirit as "love, joy, peace, patience, kindness, goodness, faithfulness, gentleness and self-control" (vv. 22–23). All of these attributes are things we *are* that flow into the things we *do*.

This concept is difficult for some to grasp. For my entire life I have placed my worth on the things I *did* instead of who I *was*. God has revealed to me through His Word that He does not view me that way; therefore, I should not view myself that way. It is a daily struggle. I am much more comfortable accepting an invitation over to a friend's house after I have done something for them to earn their friendship. The thought that I would have friends who like to be around me for who

I am makes me feel uncomfortable. God uses this to help me grow and has put friends in my life who don't really need my help but invite me to spend time with them anyway.

Our society is performance based. It is difficult to see people the way God sees them. He sees people for who they are instead of what they are doing or not doing. In Jesus' time the Pharisees believed they were "doing" the right things, but Christ often rebuked them for the hypocrisy in their hearts. Instead, He chose to surround Himself with the people who weren't *doing* the right things but were trying to *be* the right people. Maintaining our own focus on this purpose will help each of us as individuals "to act justly and to love mercy and to walk humbly with your God."

Jesus focused a lot of His teaching on having the right attitude. He didn't focus on the murderer but on the one who is angry at his brother. He didn't focus on the adulterer but on the one who looked lustfully. Christ rebuked the Pharisees who were doing all the right things but had the wrong attitudes. It is easy to fall into the same trap. Often we start with the right motives and attitude but then focus on the chore of doing instead of the joy of being.

First Peter 1:15–16 says: "But just as he who called you is holy, so be holy in all you do; for it is written: 'Be holy, because I am holy.'"

What does it mean to be holy? At first glance this seems like an impossible task, particularly when compared with Almighty God. This verse refers back to Leviticus 11 where God is providing the boundaries and regulations of the law to the Israelites to keep them distinct from other people. That is the context and meaning of the word *holy*; it means "to be set apart." This is where we derive the concept of sanctification from Scripture. As a church we are sanctified to be the bride of Christ. This should make the church a people group different from any social club or society. The church is meant to be a body of believers with a unified love and purpose for God's glory.

In the same way we as individual believers are to be sanctified or set apart from the world. This doesn't mean we should isolate ourselves from society, but we should be fundamentally different in our thought processes, actions, speech, etc. The key here is again the word *be*. Our lives must represent a change in us that is both internal and eternal—change that is so dramatic it is evident in us for the rest of our lives. It is the change that distinguishes the sheep from the goats. If we reexamine Matthew 25, we see that the lost (goats) appear to be somewhat surprised at their fate. This is confirmed in Matthew 7:21–23 where Jesus says: "Not everyone who says to me 'Lord, Lord' will enter the kingdom of heaven, but only he who does the will of my Father who is in heaven. Many will say to me on that day, 'Lord, Lord, did we not prophesy in your name, and in your name drive out demons and perform many miracles?' Then I will tell them plainly, 'I never knew you. Away from me, you evildoers!'"

This passage clearly communicates that God is not looking for us to *do* as much as He is looking for us to *be*. This is because the doing will flow from the being. The people in this passage were *doing* what they thought were good things; they were prophesying and performing miracles in Jesus' name, but they lacked the true relationship. They lacked the *being*. They were focused on the works instead of being focused on the person who will naturally exude those same works. The things we do can be blessed or forgiven, but the person we are determines if we are saved or condemned.

You don't need to teach a child how to imagine. A child will imagine because he or she is a child. You don't need to tell a mother to defend her child. She will naturally do so because she is a mother. You shouldn't have to tell a Christian to act like Christ. The outflow should be a reflection of the person inside. "Jesus replied: "'Love the Lord your God with all your heart and with all your soul and with all your mind.' This is the first and greatest commandment. And the second is like it: 'Love your neighbor as yourself'"" (Matt. 22:37–39).

In this Scripture, Jesus commands us to love. Love should flow from who we are as believers in Jesus as our Lord and Savior. The command should be part of our nature, not a burden. We expect a joyful person to smile or a fearful person to worry; it is an outward sign of who they are. Similarly, the command to love is really a command to show an outward sign of who we are. "By this all men will know that you are my disciples, if you love one another" (John 13:35).

Purpose should flow from being what God desires us to be and should match with our principle and position. In His wisdom God put us in a certain place at a certain time for a certain purpose, to be witnesses for the praise of His glory. When we *are* what we are supposed to be, we will *do* what we are supposed to do. "Blessed is the man who does not walk in the counsel of the wicked or stand in the way of sinners or sit in the seat of mockers. But his delight is in the law of the LORD, and on his law he meditates day and night. He is like a tree planted by streams of water, which yields its fruit in season and whose leaf does not wither. Whatever he does prospers" (Ps. 1:1–3).

This is a powerful psalm that describes the man I want to be and the man I want to be remembered as. Note the action verbs in the beginning of this passage. This Scripture begins with listing the actions we are not to do ("does not walk . . . with the wicked," stand with sinners, sit with mockers). When contrasting with the actions we are not to do, the psalmist describes a character trait (whose delight is in the law of the Lord) that yields an action (mediates on His law day and night). The remainder of this description of a righteous man lists character traits that stem from a life of *being* ("yields fruit in . . . season," "leaf does not wither," "prospers").

Ultimately, isn't that what we all want? We all want to bear fruit, to remain strong, and to prosper in what we do. The key to fulfilling purpose again falls back on delighting in the principle of God's Word.

Several analogies in Scripture use the phrase "bear fruit" as a description of a natural outcome of life. Throughout Paul's epistles he often expresses his desire to see the church bear fruit.

And this is my prayer: that your love may abound more and more in knowledge and depth of insight, so that you may be able to discern what is best and may be pure and blameless until the day of Christ, filled with the fruit of righteousness that comes through Jesus Christ—to the glory and praise of God. (Phil. 1:9–11)

We have not stopped praying for you and asking God to fill you with the knowledge of his will through all spiritual wisdom and understanding. And we pray this in order that you may live a life worthy of the Lord and please him in every way: bearing fruit in every good work, growing in the knowledge of God. (Col. 1:9–10)

In the book of John, chapter 15, Jesus talks at length about the requirements to bear fruit: "I am the vine; you are the branches. If a man remains in me and I in him, he will bear much fruit; apart from me you can do nothing" (v. 5).

Isaiah 11 has a prophecy about Jesus as One who will come from the line of David bearing fruit: "A shoot will come up from the stump of Jesse; from his roots a Branch will bear fruit" (v. 1).

So what exactly does it mean to "bear fruit"?

Many of these scriptural references pertain to two aspects of fruit. The first is the consumable function of fruit and is often correlated to the spiritual fruit of Galatians 5: "But the fruit of the Spirit is love, joy, peace, patience, kindness, goodness, faithfulness, gentleness and self-control" (vv. 22–23).

When a believer is living according to God's will and purpose, this fruit is a natural result of the person they are. Who doesn't like being around someone who is loving, joyful, peaceful, and kind? This outward fruit is a sign of an inward spiritual condition just as a grape is an outward sign of a grapevine. The grapevine, to fulfill its purpose, will not produce anything except grapes.

The other aspect of fruit is that it contains a seed. The seed of the fruit is used to produce more plants of the same kind. "The fruit of the righteous is a tree of life, and he who wins souls is wise" (Prov. 11:30).

A believer who is living according to God's purpose should be producing other believers of the same kind. This aspect of bearing fruit points to discipleship and sharing with others what you believe. Not to do so would make you a seedless grape. You look like you came from the grapevine, but you cannot reproduce as God intended.

If I am convinced the Bible is the only principle on which to base life and it offers truth in position and purpose, and if I really love others, then I must share my convictions. I must care about the souls of other people, not out of obligation but out of love. I must desire to bear fruit and see others change position from lost to saved. I must long for others to find the satisfaction and purpose in life that I have found. Some will accept and discover purpose. Others will not accept. Those that reject God still have a destiny but do not have a fulfilling purpose.

Second Peter 3:9 states that God does "not [want] anyone to perish, but everyone to come to repentance." God doesn't create people who have no hope of a purpose, but each of us is responsible to seek out that purpose based on our principle and position.

What is your purpose?

Dan's Story

Dan's friend John was a lot like Dan but much older. They met when Dan was working his way through college, and they stayed in touch periodically even after Dan graduated and moved on. John worked hard all his life and retired in the peaceful countryside. He was a talented mechanic and had a love for old cars. John purchased a classic car that needed a lot of work.

It was the dream car he would often tell Dan about when they worked together. Feeling a bit empty since his retirement, John spent all day every day rebuilding his classic car. He seemed happy as he searched the Internet for parts and meticulously assembled each component.

Time and distance started separating their friendship, but Dan still tried to call John a couple times a year to stay in touch. John would tell him all about his latest find or how much he had completed on his car. Dan was moderately interested in John's car but felt a bit awkward during their conversations because the car was all John wanted to talk about. Dan tried to tell John about the investments he was making in his family and his church, but John didn't seem interested. At one point Dan asked John what he was going to do with the car when it was finished. John was silent for a few moments as if he had never really thought that far in advance. "I don't know, Dan. I just don't know."

Chapter 9

PASSION

Each of us has a natural inclination or drive. It is ingrained in our being. Some are driven to be athletes while others are driven to be actors, scientists, or teachers. Passion is what drives us to do the things we love to do. It is the job we would do regardless of pay or benefits. It is the event we get excited about. It is the subject we love talking about. It is the hobby we want to invest our resources in. Passion is the fuel that makes the automobile move or the wind that pushes the sailboat through the water.

Passion exists in two forms. First is natural passion, which is something you are born with. Some people have a natural love for drama and excitement while others may have a natural passion for research and stability. The second form of passion is developed and nurtured. You may not have a natural passion for recycling, but if it fits with your principle to be environmentally responsible, then you can develop and nurture such a passion. The passions that match with your principle are easy to develop. If you have ever tried to develop a passion for something and it became too cumbersome, it was likely not lined up with your principle, position, or purpose.

Like position, passion should be based on principle and should coincide with purpose. Passion without the correct principle can be dangerous. Many radical extremist religions and cult groups embrace passion without the right principle. It is evident in the Nazi soldiers of World War II. They were extremely passionate about their cause, as were the Islamic terrorists who attacked the World Trade Center in New York. These and others were firmly committed to their cause and were pursuing their purpose as it aligned to their principle. While we, too, are called to a passion and a purpose, it must be aligned with the right principle.

Passion should be the fuel that equips us to fulfill our purpose. In most cases our passion aligns with our talents. We are each given specific talents, gifts, and abilities that God desires to work through for the praise of His glory and for our own personal growth. It makes sense that we should exercise those gifts to improve or enhance them. The more we nurture our passions, the better we become at using them.

My older daughter is gifted at choreography. She loves to create dance moves to songs. As unbiased as a father can be, I think she is really good at it. She doesn't need to be prompted to do it, and she can often be found in her room listening to a song over and over again to put the right moves together in step to the beat. The more she does it, the better she becomes at it. She doesn't even know it is called choreography, but she does know that she can do it well, and it makes her happy so she continues. If she keeps exercising that talent, it can become a well-developed passion for dance.

My younger daughter is gifted at music. She didn't inherit that talent from her father. She loves to play the piano, and she plays beautifully. Piano practice for her is fun and exciting. She loves to learn new songs and loves to play songs for others to hear. When she encounters a difficult song, she works at it until she gets it right. As she increases her skill, she is unknowingly fueling a passion for music.

You won't find many Olympic swimmers who don't love to swim or great artists who don't love to draw and paint. People naturally flourish in the areas they are talented in; it is how we are made, and it is no coincidence.

Romans 12:6–8 gives us a sampling of gifts within the church body that are meant to be exercised with passion: "We have different gifts, according to the grace given to us. If a man's gift is prophesying, let him use it in proportion to his faith. If it is serving, let him serve; if it is teaching, let him teach; if it is encouraging, let him encourage; if it is contributing to the needs of others, let him give generously; if it is leadership, let him govern diligently; if it is showing mercy, let him do it cheerfully."

Each believer has been given specific gifts, talents, and abilities that are meant to be used to fulfill our purpose in giving God glory. When we are exercising those unique gifts and talents to fulfill our purpose, it ignites a passion within us, making the duty of service more like an experience to enjoy.

Some passions are inherited or developed. A young man's passion for sports is often fueled by his father's passion for the same sport or even the same team. This is an area where we need to be mindful of what we are encouraging in our children. It is paramount for us to nurture a passion for Scripture, a passion for prayer, and a passion for a deeper relationship with God into the next generation. Following the instructions to the Israelites in Deuteronomy 6:7, it is something you should talk about "when you sit at home and when you walk along the road, when you lie down and when you get up." Basically, something we should do all the time. If our children see genuine excitement in us for seeking God and overwhelming joy in us as we use our gifts for His purpose, they, too, will likely have that desire for their own lives.

Sometimes we need to develop a passion within our own lives as well. The development of a passion often begins with a choice. When we choose to be obedient, the desire to be obedient will grow within us. You invest your time in the things you are passionate about. "For where your treasure is, there your heart will be also" (Matt. 6:21).

This verse includes the treasure of our time and focus. If I chose to invest a lot of time in my hobbies, I would become passionate about them. If I chose to invest a lot of time studying the Bible, I would be more passionate about it. If I chose to invest a lot of time in my marriage and my children, I would also become passionate about them. It is critical to develop and nurture passions that we are accountable to God for.

I have chosen to develop a passion to love my wife. Because I chose to love her, my love for her intensifies. The definition of love in today's society is kept primarily to an emotional feeling destined to fade over time. The love God calls us to through His Word is foremost a love by choice. When I choose to love my wife (even at times when she may not deserve it), then my love for her grows within me until it becomes a passion. Ephesians 5:25 and Colossians 3:19 both command husbands to love their wives. The command implies that there is a choice not to obey. If I view love as just a feeling or a chemical attraction, then I can't control when I love or do not love my wife. But since I view love on the basis of my principle, I see it as a choice and a command to be followed. The great result of following this command wholeheartedly is that it stirs a passion in me to do it more.

The message of the gospel aligns to this concept perfectly. God chose to set His heart on us. He chose to love us even though we were unlovable. We were not just unlovable, but we were mortal enemies with God because of our sin. In His divine wisdom, and beyond our capability to understand why, God made the choice. His choice was to love us and to show us love. God is so passionate about loving us that He was willing to sacrifice greatly for us.

Before the world began, God was perfectly content within Himself and needed nothing for His own satisfaction. The Bible says He created this universe and this planet for man to live on. Even before the first act of creation, God knew that man would sin and rebel from Him. Knowing that, and being a sovereign God, He could have chosen not to create us at all. He could have chosen not to give us a choice. He didn't need to put the tree of the knowledge of good and evil in the garden of Eden. The tree was placed there to give humankind the opportunity to rebel. This allowed humankind the opportunity to choose God over something else. But in His plan He chose to create us. He chose to give us an opportunity to rebel, knowing that we would. He chose to make the only form of redemption the sacrifice of Jesus on a cross. Why did God make those choices? The answer is in both of the following passages: "But God demonstrates his own love for us in this: While we were still sinners, Christ died for us" (Rom. 5:8). "This is how we know what love is: Jesus Christ laid down his life for us" (1 John 3:16).

God chose to love us. Not only did He choose to love us, but He also chose to show us what love really is. It was His choice, and that choice reflects His passion to love us. We never deserved it, and we can never repay it.

Let's return to the passage in Ephesians: "Praise be to the God and Father of our Lord Jesus Christ, who has blessed us in the heavenly realms with every spiritual blessing in Christ. For he *chose* us in him before the creation of the world to be holy and blameless in his sight. In love he predestined us to be adopted as his sons through Jesus Christ, in accordance with his pleasure and will—to the praise of his glorious grace, which he has freely given us in the One he loves" (1:3–6, author's emphasis).

God chose to love us. Because of His love, He sacrificed for us so that we may be adopted for His glory. How could we not want to nurture a passion to know Him better?

God's plan for redemption is evidence enough that He has a passion for us, but He doesn't stop there. Romans 8:28 says that God is working out all things for good for those who love Him. He is actively involved in the daily activities of those who believe in Him. God also longs to commune with us and longs for us to grow.

I have found this concept of passion holds true in many aspects of life. The more I choose to love my wife and children, the more I am driven to continue to love them on a grander scale. The more I choose to study the Bible, the more passion I have to dig deeper into seeking God. The more I choose to pray for others, the more passion I develop for them.

Too often we view the commandments of Scripture as burdens when they should be seen as a means to fulfill our purpose. God doesn't command us to do things that are contrary to the way He designed us. When we align to His commands and choose to obey, the passion to grow will yield a much more satisfying life than we could ever provide for ourselves.

After the rule of David and Solomon, Israel began a period of division, captivity, and torment that lasts throughout history even until the present day. After Solomon's death the kingdom was divided into the northern kingdom, which was referred to as Israel being comprised of ten tribes, and the southern kingdom, referred to as Judah being comprised of the tribes of Benjamin and Judah. The northern kingdom was captured by the Assyrians. The southern kingdom, Judah, was captured by the Babylonians. During the capture of Judah, Solomon's temple was destroyed, and the walls of Jerusalem were crushed. In 583 BC, the Persians conquered Babylon and granted the people of Judah their freedom to return to their homeland. Approximately fifty thousand Judeans returned to the war-torn Jerusalem while others stayed behind in Persian territory.

The book of Nehemiah is a historical record of God's movement to restore His people back to their own land. Nehemiah was a servant to the Persian king Artaxerxes. More specifically, he was the king's cupbearer. The job of the cupbearer was to serve drinks at the royal table. The cupbearer was also responsible for ensuring that the royal drinks were not poisoned and often was required to taste the wine prior to serving it. The position was highly respected in the royal court, and Nehemiah had a good reputation with the king.[5]

In the first chapter of the book of Nehemiah, his brother, Hanani, returned from Jerusalem to give Nehemiah a disturbing report about the condition of their homeland. More specifically, he told Nehemiah the city of Jerusalem was vulnerable to attack as the walls had been torn down and the gates burned. This news coupled with Nehemiah's love for Jerusalem ignited a passion within him that is evident in the rest of the book.

The effect the bad news had on Nehemiah is recorded in chapter 1: "When I heard these things, I sat down and wept. For some days I mourned and fasted and prayed before the God of heaven" (v. 4).

Nehemiah reacted with a deep passion to repair the walls of Jerusalem and help restore the people of Israel back to their home city and to a right relationship with

God. In his prayer that follows verse 4, Nehemiah's passion clearly aligns with God's will and is backed by Nehemiah's principle of God's Word: "Remember the instruction you gave your servant Moses, saying, 'If you are unfaithful, I will scatter you among the nations, but if you return to me and obey my commands, then even if your exiled people are at the farthest horizon, I will gather them from there and bring them to the place I have chosen as a dwelling for my Name'" (Neh. 1:8–9).

The intent of this prayer is not to remind God of what He had said. God does not forget. Instead Nehemiah is aligning his desires with the principle of God's word. Throughout the book, Nehemiah remains focused on alignment with God's will through prayer. Before every major milestone in his undertaking, Nehemiah prays. Nehemiah's position as the cupbearer to the king allowed him to gain the audience with the king that was necessary for him to get the resources and time necessary to fulfill his purpose of restoring the wall and the people of Israel to a right relationship with God (Neh. 1:5–11).

Rebuilding the wall of Jerusalem was a daunting task, but Nehemiah had such a deep passion that he was undeterred in his efforts. In chapter 2, we also see that his passion was contagious: "I also told them about the gracious hand of my God upon me and what the king had said to me. They replied, 'Let us start rebuild-ing.' So they began the good work" (v. 18).

In chapters 5 and 6, Scripture records some of the obstacles Nehemiah dealt with as there was much opposition to the effort. Throughout these chapters though, Nehemiah's resolve is clear. He is focused on his passion and does not waiver from completing the task with excellence.

The rebuilt wall of Jerusalem was finished in fifty-two days. Given the tools and resources of that time, completing the work in that short duration was an astonishing feat.

What began as one man's *passion* to restore the people of Israel aligned with the *principle* of God's Word. Nehemiah was in the right *position*, and that led to a definition and a fulfillment of *purpose*.

> The rest of the people—priests, Levites, gate-keepers, singers, temple servants and all who separated themselves from the neighboring peo-ples for the sake of the Law of God, together with their wives and all their sons and daughters who are able to understand—all these now join their brothers the nobles, and bind themselves with a curse and an oath to follow the Law of God given through Moses the servant of God

and to obey carefully all the commands, regulations and decrees of the LORD our Lord. (Neh.
10:28–29)

What are your passions? Are your passions aligned
with your principle? Do you need to give up some
passions in your life in order to develop and nurture
passions that are aligned with God's purpose for your
life? Are the choices you make every day consistent
with your passion, purpose, and principle? These are
all tough questions, but growing is difficult. God wants
us to use our passions freely, but we are responsible
to develop and nurture the ones that are aligned with
Scripture as our principle. In doing so, we become more
energized about our purpose. Nurturing the right passions within our own lives will become contagious to
those around us and help to make a greater impact on
others.

Dan's Story

Dan loved to work. No matter the job, Dan poured
everything he had into it. He longed to be the best at
whatever he was doing. It didn't take long for Dan's
identity to be caught up in his work; he lived and

breathed it every day. He took pride in being a hard worker, but it almost cost him a missed opportunity.

Before he met the girl who would become his wife, Dan would work twelve to fifteen hours a day at his job without a second thought. He wanted to be successful, and he was passionate about his work. Dan continued his pursuit of a successful career into the early months of the relationship with his future wife. She didn't share Dan's same enthusiasm for a successful career at all costs. They both talked about their relationship being serious, but she felt like Dan focused more on his work than on her. She was so concerned about his tendency to let his job drive his purpose that she considered ending their relationship.

After a lengthy discussion Dan promised her that he would work less as their relationship grew and that he would be there for her when she needed him. That promise soon turned into a passion to love her more each day. He held true to his word, and they got married. After the wedding and honeymoon, life got back to normal, and Dan returned to his job. He began to think of her throughout the day and longed to get home quickly after work to be with her. The more time he spent with her, the more time he wanted to spend with her. She quickly became his favorite person to be with.

Chapter

10

PERSPECTIVE

Each of us has a different perspective on life. Our individual perspectives are shaped by our experiences and circumstances. Our perspective on life is also dictated by our principle, position, and purpose. If my principle includes the theory of evolution, then my perspective on life and my belief about the purpose of life is bleak. If my principle is the Bible, then my perspective of God as a loving Father and righteous judge influences my decisions. Perspective is often a matter of choice. Your perspective can change your attitude about your circumstances and can become a major factor in how others see you.

Perspective can also be a visible indicator of spiritual and emotional maturity. Often someone's perspective in the face of tragedy reveals the true nature of that person's character.

I have met people who have gone through immense loss or have faced terminal illness but through it all maintained a deep sense of joy and contentment based on their perspective of God. We are often amazed by these types of people and sometimes long for such a deep level of faith. Naturally we want the faith without going through the trial. Unfortunately most of the time faith matures in the harshest of circumstances, and as faith matures, perspectives change.

Throughout Scripture are examples of men and women whose perspective on God was changed as their faith matured. The book of Ruth is a great example of God's changing someone's perspective to more accurately reflect His character. The story of Ruth began with a woman named Naomi. Naomi had a husband and two sons. Naomi's family lived in Bethlehem but moved to the country of Moab when a famine swept through their homeland. Moab was a nation born out of an incestuous relationship between Lot and his daughter (Gen. 19:36–37). The Moabites did not maintain a favorable relationship with the Israelites throughout the Bible. While in Moab, Naomi's two sons married Moabite women. Over the course of about ten years, Naomi's husband and both of her sons died. Disappointed in the way she felt God had treated her, Naomi decided to move back to Bethlehem, and only one of her daughters-in-law, Ruth, chose to follow her there. When she arrived back to her hometown, Naomi told all of her friends to stop calling her Naomi and to start calling her Mara which means "bitter" because she felt afflicted and wronged by God (Ruth 1:20–21).

This is a familiar story to some, but I challenge you to read it again from Ruth's perspective. Ruth fell in love and married a man from an unfriendly nation. She became a widow at a relatively young age and opted to travel to a foreign land with her mother-in-law. Ruth's perspective of God early in the book was defined by the loss of her husband and by Naomi's bitter attitude toward God. She must have thought God was cruel and unjust; still she made the right choice and remained loyal to being a provider for her mother-in-law. After Ruth and Naomi arrived in Bethlehem, God revealed himself through Boaz as the kinsmen-redeemer and saved both Ruth and Naomi from a life of poverty.

Boaz took a special interest in Ruth while she was working in his fields. He provided her with safety (Ruth

2:8–9), water (Ruth 2:9), blessing (Ruth 2:12), comfort and kindness (Ruth 2:13), bread (Ruth 2:14), and abundance (Ruth 2:16). All of these provisions parallel what God provides to us through Jesus as our Redeemer, living water and bread of life. God also blessed Ruth and Boaz with a son (Ruth 4:13–17). Ruth's son was the grandfather of King David. If she had chosen to stay in Moab, she may have never understood God as anything more than a cruel force of nature. She could have defined God through the community principle of her mother-in-law. She may have felt justified in being bitter toward God. She may have felt mistreated and unloved. Instead of focusing internally on her feelings and her circumstances, Ruth left her comfort zone to do the right thing and showed love to her mother-in-law. As a result of her choice, Ruth's perspective of God changed. Her faith in Him grew, and she became a significant person in the lineage of Jesus.

Perhaps you are reading this book and feel jaded, mistreated, or bitter toward God. Many of life's circumstances are not easy to explain, and blaming God is an easier path to take when you have been hurt. As difficult as the situation can be, it is essential that you push through life's tough circumstances and continue to make the right choices. Similar to Ruth, you may find that God uses the difficult situations in life to change your perspective on Him and to bless you in ways you cannot understand.

.Job was a righteous man who had God's hand of blessing on his life. In Job 1:8, God describes Job as "blameless and upright, a man who fears God and shuns evil." Without notice or warning, God offered Job up to Satan to be persecuted. Job lost his wealth, his children, and his health but never lost his testimony that God is forever faithful. His perspective and understanding of God deepened significantly through his trials. "My ears had heard of you but now my eyes have seen you. Therefore I despise myself and repent in dust and ashes" (Job 42:5–6).

At the end of the book, Job questioned God and established a better understanding of God's sovereignty. Through the tribulation God never explained the purpose of the test but instead used the circumstance to help Job better understand more of His character. God does not owe us an explanation for His actions or His allowances. God is much too big for us to understand. Often the only way to understand God's character better is to experience His faithfulness through tough times.

Even in the New Testament, the twelve disciples, who were the men closest to Jesus, often had a wrong perspective of God. After these men spent three years with Jesus, they accompanied Him on a journey to Jerusalem. When some of the Samaritan villages refused to welcome Jesus, the disciples became irate. After they saw years of the demonstrated love Jesus had for the people and after they heard Him talk of His purpose to redeem humankind, James and John asked Jesus if they should "call fire down from heaven to destroy them" (Luke 9:54). Jesus rebuked them for not having a correct perspective of Him and for His mission.

Of the twelve disciples Peter was the only one with enough faith to get out of the boat and walk on the water; yet he was also rebuked by Jesus several times for his impetuous actions and incorrect perspective of God. After Jesus was taken to be crucified, Peter experienced the heartbreak of denying his Lord. Peter changed his perspective after the resurrection. He refocused his life on God's plan instead of his own and became one of the greatest leaders of the early church.

Paul had a Pharisee perspective of God early in his life and had all of the right credentials to be considered spiritual in the eyes of the culture, but his perspective of God radically changed on the road to Damascus. Through his encounter with Jesus, Paul realized that his perspective of God was wrong and immediately changed his position to get a better perspective.

In December 2010, I took my oldest daughter to Peru on a mission trip. My prayer was that God would use the trip to deepen my faith, to deepen her faith, and to strengthen our relationship. My plan was to change her perspective; God's plan was to change my perspective. The first day we were there, she became sick, and we stayed behind in Lima while the rest of the mission team took the bus to Huaraz. After a day of recovery, she felt better so we went to the bus station to catch a bus to Huaraz to meet up with the rest of the team. The bus ride from Lima to Huaraz was scheduled to be an eight-hour trip. Due to a political unrest, we were stopped by several roadblocks and were forced to take a different route. We were stuck on the bus with one bottle of water, one pack of crackers, no method of communication, no fellow travelers who spoke English, and no idea where we were. I didn't know when we would get to Huaraz or even if we were still going there. After thirty hours on the bus, we ran out of food and water. We were tired, thirsty, hungry, and smelly. In the midst of that ordeal, I could not see God's purpose or sense His presence. I felt destitute. I prayed hard and begged for God to rescue us. I knew that without God's intervention, our situation was hopeless. As hard as I prayed, God remained silent. I did my part to help clear roadblocks, but I knew we were completely dependent on God. We had to trust Him even when He was silent. After thirty-five grueling hours on the bus, we arrived in Huaraz. The team welcomed us and provided us with a much-needed meal, a shower, and a nap.

Looking back on that situation, I can see where God protected us and how He used those circumstances to deepen my faith. It wasn't without some scary emotion and pain, but it was well worth it. The experience changed my perspective of God. I understand His character better now. I can also see where He answered my prayer, but He opted to do it in a way I was not expecting.

Ultimately, learning more about someone's character is part of the constantly growing relationship God desires to have with us. He already knows all of me, the good and the bad. My responsibility is to seek more of Him. Through Scripture, prayer, and circumstance, God will continue to reveal more of Himself and alter our perspective of Him as we journey in life. This growing relationship and perspective are part of our purpose.

God shares His character and His attributes throughout Scripture because He wants us to have a proper perspective of Him. He wants us to see Him as the great Redeemer in the book of Ruth and as the sovereign God of the universe in Job and as the Lord of our lives in the New Testament. God also wants us to have a proper perspective of ourselves in relation to Him.

Let's revisit the woman who touched Jesus' robe in Mark 5. I was certain I had reaped everything I needed from this passage when I wrote the chapter on the relationship principle, but then, as I was explaining it to my girls, God showed me so much more. This time let's expand the context to include the miracle of Jairus's daughter. It is a long passage, but there are some important points here so please stick with me.

> When Jesus had again crossed over by boat to the other side of the lake, a large crowd gathered around him while he was by the lake. Then one of the synagogue leaders, named Jairus, came there. Seeing Jesus, he fell at his feet and pleaded earnestly with him, "My little daughter is dying. Please come and put your hands on her so that she will be healed and live." So Jesus went with him. A large crowd followed and pressed around him. And a woman was there who had been subject to bleeding for twelve years. She had suffered a great deal under the care of many doctors and had spent all she had, yet instead of getting better she grew worse. When she heard about Jesus, she came up behind him in

the crowd and touched his cloak, because she thought, "If I just touch his clothes, I will be healed." Immediately her bleeding stopped and she felt in her body that she was freed from her suffering. At once Jesus realized that power had gone out from him. He turned around in the crowd and asked, "Who touched my clothes?"

"You see the people crowding against you," his disciples answered, "and yet you can ask, 'Who touched me?'"

But Jesus kept looking around to see who had done it. Then the woman, knowing what had happened to her, came and fell at his feet and, trembling with fear, told him the whole truth. He said to her, "Daughter, your faith has healed you. Go in peace and be freed from your suffering."

While Jesus was still speaking, some people came from the house of Jairus, the synagogue ruler. "Your daughter is dead," they said. "Why bother the teacher anymore?"

Ignoring what they said, Jesus told the synagogue ruler, "Don't be afraid; just believe."

He did not let anyone follow him except Peter, James and John the brother of James. When they came to the home of the synagogue ruler, Jesus saw a commotion, with people crying and wailing loudly. He went in and said to them, "Why all this commotion and wailing? The child is not dead but asleep." But they laughed at him.

After he put them all out, he took the child's father and mother and the disciples who were with him, and went in where the child was. He took her by the hand and said to her, *"Talitha koum!"* (which means "Little girl, I say to you, get up!"). Immediately the girl stood up and began to walk around (she was twelve years old). At this they were completely astonished. He gave strict orders not to let anyone know about this, and told them to give her something to eat. (Mark 5:21–43)

These two miracles are recorded in three of the four Gospels and are always linked together. When we look at these two miracles as they are woven together in Scripture, some interesting comparisons become evident.

First, we start with Jairus. His name means "God enlightens." Jairus was a synagogue ruler; he was an important figurehead in that time period. Jairus had a twelve-year-old daughter; in fact, the parallel passage in Luke 8 states that she was his only daughter and she was near death. One of my daughters just happens to be twelve years old right now, so this particular story has special and relatable meaning in my life. Jairus knew that apart from a miraculous healing by Jesus, his only daughter would die, and he was powerless to do anything to help her. The extent of his pleading with Jesus clearly indicates that he loved his daughter more than anything and that he didn't want her to die. I would feel the same way.

As Jesus is on His way to handle the situation, we suddenly get introduced to another character who remains nameless in the Gospel accounts. She, too, was dying—spiritually. Because of her bleeding issue and the requirements of Leviticus 15, she was considered ceremonially unclean by society and was excluded from going to the synagogue and the temple. She had spent all that she had on doctors for healing, but her situation only grew worse. She was powerless to heal herself or to change her socially unclean status. She was a daughter of God who had been slowly dying for twelve years. She didn't see herself for who she was, and she didn't see Jesus for who He really was.

As we saw in the previous chapter, this woman's perspective of Jesus was not entirely accurate. She saw Him as a great healer and as the means to fix her current problem. We can also see here that her perspective of herself was wrong. She devalued herself to the point of avoiding an interaction with Jesus. Perhaps after twelve years of being shunned by society, she had accepted herself as unworthy. Because of her faith, she was healed and in all three Gospel accounts Jesus called her a name that must have gotten her attention; He called her "Daughter." The Hebrew word used here means "daughter of God; acceptable to God." After years of rejection by society and the feeling of a slow spiritual death, this woman finally felt accepted and perhaps realized that her perspective of herself was much different from God's perspective of her.[6]

Holding true to His faithful character, Jesus commissioned the woman to "go in peace and be freed from your suffering." Not just the physical suffering but also the emotional, psychological, and spiritual suffering. The phrase "your faith has healed you" used in Matthew 9:22 can be translated "saved you." What an incredible, life-changing moment.

During this event messengers from Jairus's house arrived on the scene to deliver the bad news that his daughter had died. Can you imagine his first thoughts? He must have felt some level of despair. He may have even entertained the notion that if Jesus had not stopped for this woman, maybe they would have made it to his house in time. What Jairus didn't understand, though, is that his daughter was equally important to God as the daughter Jesus had just healed. True to his name, Jairus is about to be enlightened by God.

Jesus arrived at the house and told the people who were there that the girl was not dead but asleep. Their reaction to His statement shed light on their incorrect perspective of Him. Perhaps they thought Jesus could heal her, but was He powerful enough to bring her back from death? Certainly only God could accomplish that task. Appropriately so, Jesus "put them all out" and continued the task at hand. With only a select few witnesses, Jesus healed Jairus's daughter miraculously and completely. At this they were "completely astonished."

So many times in life, I, too, am astonished. Do I believe what the Bible says about God enough to affect my perspective of Him? Do I believe the Bible enough to shape my perspective of myself to line up with Scripture? Do I live out that perspective every day? To shape my perspective of God for who He is and my perspective of myself as a child of God, joint-heir with Christ and temple of the Holy Spirit leaves me greatly astonished.

What is your perspective of God? Is your perspective of God shaped by Scripture as the principle or by your environment or circumstances? Are you bitter with God for the bad circumstances? Do you under-stand that God is in complete control of the universe, or is your perspective only on your own little world? What is your perspective of yourself in relation to God? Does your perspective of yourself match what the Bible says about your position? What are you willing to endure to change your perspective on God? There is always more of Him to know.

Dan's Story

Throughout his life Dan has been exposed to many different perspectives of God. When he was young, Dan thought God was a distant being who offered fire insurance for people who didn't want to go to hell. Later in life Dan saw some television preachers portray God as a cosmic genie ready to grant you wishes of riches and prosperity. Apparently that view was working for them as most of them, had designer suits and shiny jewelry.

Dan's coworker, Mike, once shared how his mom died slowly and painfully of cancer despite all the prayers of his family. After that incident Mike didn't want anything to do with God. Mike clearly viewed God as some universal overlord who was indifferent and apathetic to people. Dan tried to talk to Mike about it a few times, but he refused to discuss it. His mind was made up.

Dan's old schoolmate Ron also had dismissed the thought of a relationship with God. Not because of any particular tragedy in his life but just because Ron thought believing in God was something only kids and uneducated people do. Ron had a master's degree in something Dan could never remember or properly pronounce, but it landed him a job that seemed to provide for all his desires. Ron thought God was just an imaginary being people latched onto in times of desperation. He had no need of any of it.

There were almost as many perspectives of God as there were people in Dan's life. He remembered a time in his own life when he felt like God let him fall. He wanted God to be the lifeline in a failed relationship, but despite Dan's anguish and prayer, God didn't rescue him from that ordeal. Years later Dan realized God was in control the whole time. God had something different for Dan. Something more. Something better.

PRIORITIES

The most important thing in your life is what you are spending the majority of your time, money, and energy on. The final building block in the structure of life is priorities. Priorities are defined by our principle, influenced by our position, aligned with our purpose, and affected by our passions. Priorities need to be defined and sometimes redefined when we get off track. Priorities can most easily be seen by the use of our resources because most often our resources will naturally align to our priorities.

Where are your priorities? We all know the right answers. For those who call themselves Christians, God should be the first priority, family second, and then possibly work, school, or hobbies. But does that answer really reflect where our time, money, and resources are? Can we say that God is our number-one priority when we do not study His Word, pray regularly, or acknowledge His magnificence? Can we say that God is our number one priority when our tithe is diminished or even forgotten so that we can afford our car payment, boat payment, or fund our latest hobby? In the quest for the American dream, do we give too much of our energy to our jobs instead of focusing on our purpose?

For those without a biblical principle, priorities can be difficult to manage as there is no solid standard for comparison. How do you know that you are making the most effective use of your resources? Are you spending your life doing things that are really good or just things that feel good to you? Arranging priorities based on the right principle can mean a legacy of changed lives versus the risk of becoming a fading memory. Life is too short to take that risk.

Our priorities should line up with the reality of our environment. From strictly a time line view of life, a faithfully married believer can expect to spend thirty or more years at a job, approximately fifty years in a marriage, and all of eternity with God. From the time-line perspective, God should take precedence over everything else as the most significant long-term investment; clearly our marriage relationships should fall second. The time-line perspective on life necessitates that we give God more than two hours a week and that we invest more time in our marriages than brief conversations. It is easy to put our lives in cruise control and lose focus on our own time management. Channel surfing or time spent on the Internet can too easily capture our attention, and before we realize it, hours of our lives are gone.

At one time in history the sole purpose of having a job was to provide for the needs of your family. Over time the workplace has become more. Our jobs have now turned into "careers," which can shift the focus away from priorities that are aligned with Scripture. Our careers can quickly become a means to inflate our egos and to feed our ever-growing hunger for material goods. The people who replace you at work will likely not remember your name five years after you are gone. The workplace you pour yourself into will consider you a forgotten memory, and your family will only remember your time away from them trying to climb the corporate ladder. A work-centered life is not a legacy; it is a tragedy.

In Matthew 6, Jesus provides God's perspective on priorities. "So do not worry, saying, 'What shall we eat?' or 'What shall we drink?' or 'What shall we wear?' For the pagans run after all these things, and your heavenly Father knows that you need them. But seek first his kingdom and his righteousness, and all these things will be given to you as well" (vv. 31–33).

The top priority in this verse is seeking the kingdom of God. Everything else we need will fall into place if we keep God as our first priority. Note that the "all these things" in the passage is a reference back to the necessities of life like food and clothing. The "all these things" does not include a new car, the latest smart phone, or a big-screen television.

On the opposite extreme the Bible does not tell us to forsake all other priorities. We are still accountable to work diligently, to maintain good relationships, and to fulfill our commitments. In all the things we do, we need to incorporate our purpose of glorifying God and nurturing our passions in life.

Prioritizing is not just identifying the most important area of life to focus on while ignoring everything else. Our relationship with God should be at the forefront of our resource allocation, but that doesn't mean we leave our families and our jobs to join a monastery.

We are still expected to love our spouses and prioritize them over our hobbies.

When was the last time you had a date with your spouse or surprised your spouse with something (a gift, an act of service, or a public compliment) motivated by love? We are still expected to work for our employers to the best of our ability. For most of us, our place of work represents our mission field. This is the place where the lost world gets to see our character, ethics, and personality. Are they seeing someone who sacrifices his family for his career, or are they seeing someone who works hard on the job but also has a balance in his personal life?

Priorities have a major impact on the legacy we leave. Each of us was born into this world with no resources except for the resource of time. You are responsible to dedicate your time to the right priorities. In order to commit your time, you may need to create a time allocation plan, or you may need to ask your spouse to support your renewed focus on priorities.

Acknowledging where your priorities are now and where they need to be in light of your principle is the starting point to living a life with the proper priorities. The next step is the plan to get to where you want to be. Your priority plan must include keeping God's plan and purpose as the single most important focus of your life.

Scripture provides some key instructions on keeping God as our number-one priority in all that we do. In our jobs: "Whatever you do, work at it with all your heart, as working for the Lord, not for men" (Col. 3:23).

In our life planning: "Now listen, you who say, 'Today or tomorrow we will go to this or that city, spend a year there, carry on business and make money.' Why, you do not even know what will happen tomorrow. What is your life? You are a mist that appears for a little while and then vanishes. Instead, you ought to say, 'If it is the Lord's will, we will live and do this or that'" (James 4:13–15).

In our marriages: "Husbands, love your wives, just as Christ loved the church and gave himself up for her" (Eph. 5:25).

Prioritizing God and seeking His purpose and plan for life helps us improve our quality of life by revealing what our true focus should be. Setting biblical priorities will also enhance performance in other areas of life. When my relationship with God is right, then my relationship with my wife and children is better. When my relationship with God is right, then my performance and attitude at work is better. Revisiting Psalm 1: "Blessed is the man who does not walk in the counsel of the wicked or stand in the way of sinners or sit in the seat of mockers. But his delight is in the law of the LORD, and on his law he meditates day and night. He is like a tree planted by streams of water, which yields its fruit in season and whose leaf does not wither. Whatever he does prospers" (Ps. 1:1–3).

God knows our hearts. He knows that we long to prosper and be successful. The problem is that we have defined the word *prosper* as having more stuff when the real meaning of the word is associated with balanced success. Balanced success means succeeding as an employee *and* as a husband or wife *and* as a father or mother. Prospering is not the success of one at the expense of everything else.

Second, aligning our priorities with Scripture will reveal where our idols are. What are we choosing instead of spending time with God? What are we choosing instead of reading the Bible? Is it television? Is it sports? Is it shopping? Is it the Internet? We must be intentional about prioritizing our time. The same can be true of our finances. If you say that God is your first priority, are you tithing? How much are your hobbies costing you? Americans spend more money on entertainment than any other country in the world. Where is your money going?

My wife and I have followed a budget for years, but just recently we have decided to do more detailed tracking of where the money is going. I recommend that everyone have some tracking method for their money to ensure that it aligns with their priorities. After all, "where your treasure is, there your heart will be also" (Matt. 6:21).

Solomon was King David's son. He wrote more than three thousand proverbs and was considered the wisest man who ever lived. He was also the wealthiest king of Israel. Solomon was also a pioneer in the pursuit of happiness. Solomon was the author of the book of Ecclesiastes, which chronicles Solomon's quest for satisfaction in his endeavors. He chased wisdom and knowledge (Eccles. 1:12–18). He chased pleasure and riches (Eccles. 2:1–11). He had the time and resources to chase everything the world tells us will bring satisfaction; yet he labeled it all as meaningless. At the end of the book, here is Solomon's conclusion: "Now all has been heard; here is the conclusion of the matter: Fear God and keep his commandments, for this is the whole duty of man" (Eccles. 12:13).

Who gets your best? It is a great question. Are we giving the best of ourselves to our highest priorities? Is our allocation of time, money, and talent an accurate representation of our priorities? Without a continued focus and reevaluation, our priorities can really get off track. With so many things in our culture competing for our time and attention, it can be easy to lose focus. What is your priority structure? If it is not aligned to the principle and purpose of your life, then it needs to change.

Dan's Story

Mondays at the office always seemed to be terrible. One particular Monday was an especially busy day for Dan. Piles of papers covered his desk, and his e-mail was bulging with unread messages. It seemed like everyone else had worked through the weekend to collectively execute a massive paperwork attack on Dan. His initial response was panic, but he soon regained his focus and started chipping away at the mountain of work.

A knock on the office door distracted his attention from his computer screen, and he motioned for Jim to come in. While Dan and Jim talked about a project they were working on, Dan's phone was ringing almost constantly. Each time it rang, he would glance over at the caller ID momentarily but continued his conversation with Jim. Two more people lined up outside his office door to get a word with Dan. Knowing that Dan was obviously behind and feeling the pressure of folks behind him wanting to speak to Dan was making Jim a bit nervous, but Dan maintained his calm composure. Suddenly the phone rang once again. Dan checked the caller ID and then asked Jim to be excused.

"Sure," Jim said as he got up from his chair, "but why this call? You ignored all the others."

"This one is my wife," Dan replied, "There is a difference between urgent and important."

Chapter 12

Our Model

God is so much better to us than we deserve. He gave us His written Word as the principle to live by. He gave each of us a distinct position and a specific purpose. He has provided us with the ability to develop and live our passions. He has given us the choice to set our priorities. In all of His actions, He never forces Himself on anyone. He never uses His power and ability to take hostile control of our lives without warrant. In all of this, He provides a way for us to have life abundantly. In addition, He gives us a model to follow.

Our model is the life of Jesus. In His thirty-three years on this earth, we only have highlights of His three-and-a-half-year ministry recorded for us in the Bible; yet this seemingly small amount of information can easily give us enough to study and emulate for the rest of our lives. According to Acts 11:26, the followers of Jesus in the city of Antioch were the first disciples called by the name "Christian," which means a follower of Christ. The word *Christian* in our society today means something different from what it meant in biblical times. Many of the original Christians were such dedicated followers that their characters and actions were indistinguishable from the character and actions of Jesus. The modern-day definition of the word *Christian* has been diluted to include anyone claiming to be a follower of Jesus regardless of Christlike character and actions.

God deserves more than what the modern-day Christian is willing to sacrifice. God deserves followers who know His Word. He deserves followers who know their position and purpose. He deserves followers who have the right priorities, passion, and perspective.

Before Jesus began His ministry, He was tempted by Satan. His responses to the three temptations show that Jesus knew His principle, position, and purpose.

The account of the temptation of Jesus is recorded in Luke 4.

After being in the wilderness for forty days, the Bible says Jesus was hungry. "The devil said to him, 'If you are the Son of God, tell this stone to become bread.' Jesus answered, 'It is written: "Man does not live on bread alone"'" (Luke 4:3–4). In Christ's response to Satan, He is quoting Deuteronomy 8:3. The phrase after the verse is critical to the meaning of Jesus' response: "Man does not live on bread alone but on every word that comes from the mouth of the LORD" (Deut. 8:3).

After fasting in the wilderness, Jesus still placed preeminence on the Word of God being His sustenance. It was the sole principle from which He lived. Throughout His recorded ministry Jesus quoted the Old Testament more than seventy-five times. From an early age Jesus demonstrated a deep understanding of Scripture (Luke 2:46–47). His knowledge of Scripture was intimate, real, and applicable.

The second temptation in Luke 4 was one of power and authority. Satan offered Christ authority over all of the kingdoms of the world if Jesus would bow down and worship him. Jesus knew His position. He had the power to take the authority away from Satan at any time but instead chose to be submissive to the Father's purpose for His life. Jesus knew His position as Creator and as Ruler over the universe, but He also knew that during the time of His first incarnation, His position was not to be that of divine ruler. He came to be the sin sacrifice for humankind. His future position would grant Him authority over all the kingdoms of the world, but for that time and that place, He was to fulfill God's purpose in the redemptive work of the cross.

The third temptation questions Christ's authority when Satan led Him to the highest point on the temple in Jerusalem and demanded that He prove Himself to be the Son of God by jumping off. Again, Jesus could have summoned a legion of angels to protect and defend Him, but that was not His purpose. Choosing to take His rightful place of honor and power at that time would have destined all of humankind for destruction. Jesus knew He was sent as a sacrifice for our sin. He was focused on His purpose with complete surrender to God's will.

Through His life, as recorded in Scripture, Jesus also demonstrated His passion for being obedient to the Father and for helping the helpless. He was and still is passionate about making relational connections and about glorifying God through attitudes and actions. Christ's passion is seen throughout His ministry, but it is strongest at the crucifixion. Knowing the pain and suffering He was to endure, Jesus still went willingly to the cross, driven by His passionate love for us.

Job 7:17 says, "What is man that you make so much of him, that you give him so much attention?" God has set His heart on us not because He must and not out of obligation; He chooses to. He chose to set His heart on us before the creation of the world. God has demonstrated His love and mercy throughout history, and He continues today to change lives and answer prayers.

Christ was also focused on His priorities. Clearly Jesus' priority was to glorify God and accomplish His purpose. Christ's priority of obedience is best seen in His prayer before the crucifixion: "Going a little farther, he fell with his face to the ground and prayed, 'My Father, if it is possible, may this cup be taken from me. Yet not as I will, but as you will'" (Matt. 26:39).

Jesus knew the suffering He was about to endure. He had known the plan since the beginning of time. His anguish in the moment caused drops of blood to collect on His brow; yet still He was focused on being the sacrifice God had required. In love Jesus chose to set aside His position of power to fulfill His purpose. Jesus was intentional about everything He did and every word He said. Unfortunately this is in stark contrast to how we live our routine lives today. Much of our focus is going through the motions and saying whatever pops into our heads. Christ's ministry provides insight into the character of God and provides a model for us to emulate in our own lives.

The pastor at my church is a good pastor. He preaches the Word without apology and longs for a revival in our nation. What makes him a great pastor is that he models his life after the greatest pastor there ever was. Jesus knew how to deliver God's message and how to live it out daily. He was firm when He needed to be firm and gentle when He needed to be gentle. He offered a model for all pastors to live out life's structure.

I know people who have a talent for telling stories. In His life Jesus used parables and stories to communicate God's plan for people's lives. The stories Jesus told are rich with truth and intriguing enough to be studied and researched. Through Jesus' parables we have a greater understanding of God's eternal plan and the purpose of His kingdom. Through those stories Jesus gives us an example of how to communicate His love and His plan to others. When the good storytellers of today model their lives after Christ, they become great storytellers using their talents to fulfill a strong purpose in life.

In addition to a pastor or a storyteller, many career paths can be modeled after God. He is:

- A doctor (Luke 7:22)
- An engineer (Ps. 139:13)
- A public defender (John 8:2–11)
- A craftsman (Matt. 13:55)
- A teacher (Mark 1:22)
- A financial advisor (Matt. 6:19–20)

Many of our vocational passions can and should be modeled after the character of God. This is intentional on His part. He provides us with the perfect example of Himself on how to live a purposeful life.

Christ's example doesn't stop at vocation. He was the greatest friend, counselor, provider, healer, and teacher the world would ever encounter. There is no denying His impact on every person He met. There is no escaping His influence on people and His command for us to do the same. In His final words to His followers before He ascended to heaven, Jesus gave them a command to "go and make disciples of all nations" (Matt. 28:19). The command He gave is exactly what He modeled to His followers while He was with them. It is a picture of the passing of responsibility from teacher to student. In essence Jesus is saying, "You saw what I was; now go and be that too. You saw how I did it; now go and do it also."

A study of His life reveals that Jesus knew His principle. When He was twelve years old, He stayed behind in the temple to sit among the teachers and ask questions. His thorough knowledge of the Old Testament was evident in His teachings, and He spoke as "one who had authority" (Matt. 7:29). In John 12:49, Jesus said, "For I did not speak of my own accord, but the Father who sent me commanded me what to say and how to say it." Do you know your principle? Do you know it well?

Jesus knew His position. He came to serve, teach, and save. Jesus knew His place as omniscient and Almighty God of the universe who made himself "nothing, taking the very nature of a servant, being made in human likeness" (Phil. 2:7). In John 8:14, "Jesus answered, 'Even if I testify on my own behalf, my testimony is valid, for I know where I came from and where I am going. But you have no idea where I come from or where I am going.'" Do you know your position? Do you know where you are and where you are going?

Jesus knew His purpose. He came to heal those who were sick. He "came to seek and to save what was lost" (Luke 19:10). He came to glorify the Father. In John 12:27–28, Jesus, speaking of His impending death, said, "Now my heart is troubled, and what shall I say? 'Father, save me from this hour'? No, it was for this very reason I came to this hour. Father, glorify your name!" Do you know your purpose? Are you living your purpose?

Jesus knew His passion. He came to complete God's work of redemption. "God demonstrates his own love for us in this: While we were still sinners, Christ died for us" (Rom. 5:8). Jesus' passion led Him to go to the extreme in His obedience. Do you know your passion? What do you fuel with your passion?

Jesus knew His perspective. He knew God the Father in the most intimate way possible. He had deeper insight into God's character and personality than anyone on earth, and He was eager to share that perspective in His teachings. Jesus saw His mission from the perspective of a servant: "Just as the Son of Man did not come to be served, but to serve, and to give his life as a ransom for many" (Matt. 20:28) and from the perspective of Almighty God: "All authority in heaven and on earth has been given to me" (Matt. 28:18). What is your perspective on God? Is your perspective really based on what the Bible says about God?

Jesus knew His priorities. He was sent by God to proclaim the good news. He was doubted by His own family and unwelcome in His own hometown, yet He never wavered from fulfilling God's plan. Before His death on the cross, Jesus prayed to God the Father saying, "Not my will, but yours be done" (Luke 22:42). When teaching His disciples how to pray, Jesus also focuses on the will of God: "Your will be done on earth as it is in heaven" (Matt. 6:10). Do you know your priorities? Are you living out the right priorities?

The life-structure concepts are not difficult. There is no magic formula here, but looking at the concepts and how they fit into life will help you understand the importance of knowing what you believe and why you believe it. Understanding your purpose and position will allow you to set goals of where you want to be. Maintaining your passion and priorities for the things of God allows you to become more like Jesus in your character, thoughts, and actions. Everything you need is here. The answers are here.

We have God's Word in written form, available and understandable in several translations. We have the Holy Spirit to prompt us and guide us from within. We have constant access to the throne of God through prayer. We have the life of Jesus as our model for fulfilling purpose. All of these resources are at your disposal. With these resources you can live a purposeful and satisfying life. The choice is yours. What will you do with these resources?

Dan's Story

Dan loved playing with his kids. One particular day the weather was rainy, and they were playing with building blocks. It was one of his favorite toys. Dan really enjoyed making different vehicles and buildings, and his children were impressed with his capability. The unique designs came naturally to him. As they built houses and cars, one of his daughters looked up into his eyes and, with a big smile on her face, said, "You're a great daddy and a great builder." He glanced back at her face with a smile just as big as hers.

Dan learned a lot about God's character by being a father. He also learned a lot about God by watching the world around him. Nature worked in such harmony and with such precision. Everything he saw in nature seemed to have a purpose and was beautifully crafted to fulfill that purpose. That day playing with his kids, Dan realized that not only was God a great Father; He is also a great builder.

Chapter

13

WHAT IF I AM WRONG?

T here are many schools of thought on the purpose of life and the role we play in it. I can't even begin to pretend to have all the answers. I am asking you to question your principle and measure your principle against some critical requirements, so I must be willing to do the same. I am asking you to reason out your principle and study it enough to be confident in what you believe, so I must be willing to do this as well. While I am confident in what I believe, I am asking you to be open-minded and consider the options, so I must be willing to do the same. I must ask myself the question, "What if I am wrong?"

What I believe, and what I have written in this book, takes a level of faith. *Faith* sounds like a spiritual word, but in essence it really means "confidence or trust in a person or thing" or "being certain of the things we hope for." *Faith* means "to believe wholeheartedly." Faith, though, is not limited to scriptural beliefs. It takes a great deal of faith to believe the human race is evolved from microorganisms with no documented evidence of the evolutionary process. Humankind has inhabited the earth for thousands of years, yet no one has conclusive scientific proof that evolution occurs. Evolution does not happen in today's world, and there are no accurate fossil records of an animal in mid-evolutionary process.

It takes a great deal of faith to believe the earth was accidentally formed from a random collection of unformed matter in space. Matter or energy suddenly appearing from nowhere has not occurred since the inception of the Big Bang theory. It takes a level of faith to believe in anything that cannot be seen or proven. No single theory can be scientifically proven with complete accuracy. All theories require faith.

What we choose to believe, our principle, shapes the way we live our lives and molds our view of ourselves and our environment. Because I believe in God and because I believe the Bible is God's inerrant Word, I live my life according to the standards of the Bible. I believe I have a purpose. I believe my purpose is to serve and glorify God. I believe I have a responsibility to love other people and to avoid doing things that would hurt someone else. I believe I have the privilege to love and stay true to my wife. I believe everyone, including me, will be judged according to what they have done during their life on this earth. I have a full life that is rewarding. I have a deep sense of purpose and a passion to live for.

I teach my girls that they also have a purpose to fulfill. I teach them that they are created and loved by an awesome God who will always protect them, even when I am not there to protect them myself. I teach them to use their passion to fuel their purpose. I teach them to understand and fulfill their purpose with the right perspective of themselves, God, and others. They become my legacy. I hope they will reap the same rewards I have and more. I hope their lives will be as rewarding as mine has been. I hope they will feel complete in their purpose.

So, if I am wrong, then I will live a worthwhile life as a contributor to the good of society, and then one day I will die. If I am wrong, I die and become nothing, never knowing I was wrong. I won't feel stupid or regret having my beliefs because I won't exist. Either way, I left a legacy with my children and the lives I impacted. I will have inspired others to have a sense of purpose and meaning. I will be viewed by others as a benefit to society.

If I am wrong, my children will live believing they are special and have a purpose in life. Others in my life will be better for having known me. People I impacted will strive to improve and fulfill their purpose as well. Humankind will go on.

But, if I am right, then all of the aforementioned benefits still hold true. In addition, I will go to heaven when I die to spend eternity with God. I will be able to see my wife and children again. I will see the people I was able to impact in life. I will see the people who positively impacted my life. I will share eternity with friends and family. I will continue to fulfill my purpose for all of eternity.

So that is me. What about those who don't believe in God or the Bible? If they are right, then perhaps this planet is just an accident and humankind is nothing more than an evolved animal. If they are right, then every person has nothing more to look forward to when they die than six feet of dirt and a box. People can try to maintain an order of society with laws, but to what end? There is no absolute moral standard and no hope for anything beyond death.

A life based on the belief that man is nothing more than a higher form of animal with no hope of anything beyond death is a depressing existence. If they are right, then there is no legacy of hope to leave to the next generation. If they are right, there is no deeper motivation to stay true to one's spouse or to be a contributor to society. People are only really accountable to themselves and the laws of the land. That doesn't sound like a satisfying life. Worse yet, if they are wrong, then there is an eternity of consequences and regret. They will never have the opportunity to know the God they denied.

If I am right, then everyone will give an account for what they believe during their time here on earth. If I am right, then those who do not believe in the God of the Bible will spend an eternity separated from the love of God, an eternity spent in anguish and torment. "But the cowardly, the unbelieving, the vile, the murderers, the sexually immoral, those who practice magic arts, the idolaters and all liars—their place will be in the fiery lake of burning sulfur" (Rev. 21:8).

Is it worth the risk?

Each of us choose to base our life on some principle whether we realize it or not. If you had a chance to make life better and more fulfilling, would you? If you could discover your purpose and live out your passions, would you? If you had an opportunity to impact someone's life, would you?

Inherently we know there is more to life than what modern-day scientists can explain. Evidence throughout history and with primitive tribes found throughout the world today indicates that most people groups have had some concept of a supreme being governing life.

The presence of human compassion is evidence that we believe it is good to help others even at great cost to ourselves. If life was really survival of the fittest, we would be a much less compassionate culture. Cities and nations impacted by earthquakes or floods would be considered nothing more than unfortunate victims of a changing environment. The reality is that when tragedy strikes, we respond. People help. People willingly give their money, their time, and their resources to help others in need. Compassion is driven by an inherent hope that humankind is more than just an evolved animal. We have a longing to impact lives for the better. We want to leave a legacy for the next generation.

The greatest lie we will ever encounter is the lie we tell ourselves. We convince ourselves that we already know what we need to satisfy us. We convince ourselves that chasing the next material possession will fulfill us. We convince ourselves that winning the lottery will make us happier. We convince ourselves that our relationship with God is good enough as it is. We convince ourselves that we cannot control our destiny in life. All of these are lies.

There is more about the truth to be learned. There is more about your purpose to be found, and there is more of God to know. It is your responsibility to search and to study. It is your responsibility to maintain your focus and discover your purpose. It is your responsibility to set and maintain your priorities. It is not easy because life is not easy, but these responsibilities are required to leave a legacy. You choose your beliefs. You choose the type of legacy you will leave. How do you want people to remember you? Make the choice.

Dan's Story

Dan has had a busy life. He has been working hard to provide for his family and partnering with his wife to raise their children. He always seems to be involved in some type of project and is rarely seen with idle hands. Yet with all that is going on, Dan still takes time every so often to reflect on his life. He recognizes that God has blessed him with more than he could ever have imagined.

LIFE BEYOND LIVING

He has friends both in the past and some in the present that don't understand his beliefs or the change God made in him or his choices, but there is one point about Dan that cannot be argued: he loves his life. Dan has come a long way from being the little boy with no self-confidence. He goes through life's ups and downs just like the rest of us, but he has an unwavering hope. It is a hope that he wants to share with his family and friends. It is a hope that he wants to pass down to his children.

Dan prays consistently that God will use him to impact the lives of others. He prays with conviction because he really wants to make a difference, but when God answered in an unexpected way, it caught him by surprise.

Chapter

14

THE LIFE

What is life? That question spurred me to research and to study the concept of life. The search for the meaning of life drove me to break it down into a structure in order to find fulfillment in my own life and to provide direction for the lives of my children. This book is the result of my study and part of the legacy I leave for my kids.

Life is not defined by a society that rallies to save the trees and stray dogs yet kills more than one million unborn babies each year. Life is not defined by the celebrities our society worships who often are more confused and misguided than we are. Life is not defined by scientists, politicians, or the media. Life is defined by the One Acts 3:15 calls "the author of life." Life is defined by the One who calls Himself the "life": "Jesus answered, 'I am the way and the truth and the life'" (John 14:6).

Life is not wholly defined as the opposite of death. Physically, to be dead is to be without physical life, but spiritually to be dead is to be without the spiritual life of Jesus. Spiritually dead is the condition that describes everyone who does not have a relationship with God.

> As for you, you were dead in your transgressions and sins, in which you used to live when you followed the ways of this world and of the ruler of the kingdom of the air, the spirit who is now at work in those who are disobedient. All of us also lived among them at one time, gratifying the cravings of our sinful nature and following its desires and thoughts. Like the rest, we were by nature deserving of wrath. But because of his great love for us, God, who is rich in mercy, made us alive with Christ even when we were dead in transgressions—it is by grace you have been saved. (Eph. 2:1–5)

If you trust in Scripture as your principle and confess Jesus Christ as Lord and Savior, then the life you
will have after this life is a utopia existence without the
curse of sin, similar to the original design of the garden
of Eden.

The Bible begins in Genesis 2 and ends in Revelation
22 with mention of the "tree of life": "In the middle of
the garden were the tree of life and the tree of the
knowledge of good and evil" (Gen. 2:9). "On each side
of the river stood the tree of life, bearing twelve crops
of fruit, yielding its fruit every month" (Rev. 22:2).

These trees mentioned in the Bible offer life and
healing, but they are ties to more than just physical life.
The existence of the tree of life is found only before the
fall of man into sin and after sin is abolished when the
new paradise is set on earth. The tree represents life
in communion with God's presence. It represents life
with clear, unobstructed purpose. This is the life that
awaits those who live this life with Jesus as their Lord
and Savior. "To him who overcomes, I will give the right
to eat from the tree of life, which is in the paradise of
God" (Rev. 2:7).

The word *overcomes* is used in all seven letters to
the churches in Revelation. The word means "holding fast to one's faith even unto death." It is a journey
shaped by the choices we make every day. Holding true

to our beliefs requires focus and perseverance. There are many examples of people in the Bible and through-out history that started strong but did not finish well. In a marathon it is not how well you run the twenty-five miles that counts as much as how well you run the last mile. Standing firm on the Bible as the life principle and growing in a relationship with God is the path to a fulfilling life beyond the one we have now.

The purpose of this book is to address this life because what we do with this life determines the future life we will have. It isn't about paying misery dues now to have a better life later. It is about finding the passion and purpose in this life to make it satisfying and rewarding.

Jesus said, "I have come that they may have life, and have it to the full" (John 10:10). Jesus promised life abundantly for His followers. This shouldn't be interpreted as having everything we want; that is not what He is promising. He is providing an opportunity for a life of satisfaction within the context of a life that is constantly growing closer to God. It is an individual choice that requires action. We must daily determine the path we want to travel.

There are two periods of life: the life we have now on earth and the life we will have after we die. Scripture gives us insight into both. If you study the

Bible as your principle and follow the instructions and examples Scripture provides, you can fulfill your purpose and live a satisfying life. You can have a relationship with the One who designed you. You can impact others and leave a legacy for generations.

"But these are written that you may believe that Jesus is the Christ, the Son of God, and that by believing you may have life in his name" (John 20:31). A fulfilling and purposeful life can be found. It is not reserved for a select few, but it is a choice for each individual. For too long we have allowed ministers and preachers to be held to the expectation that they are the sole executors of what the Bible says. Too long we have pushed off our responsibilities to study and know the Word of God. Too long we have failed to seek for our purpose and passion for life within the confines of Scripture.

By occupation I am an engineer. I don't have a seminary degree, and I am not an ordained minister. What I do have is a passion for truth and a passion to make a difference in the world. I want life. I want a life that is pleasing to my Creator. I want a life that impacts other people. I want a life full of purpose, passion, and proper perspective and priorities. I want to leave a legacy for my children so they, too, can discover their purpose and live their passions. What do you want?

Dan's Story

Dan is an ordinary guy following an extraordinary God on the journey of life. As he studies and grows, he learns more about himself, his life, and the world around him every day. During his study of the Bible, Dan started putting together what he thought were critical components of life so he could better understand how it all worked and how he could get the most out of life.

Dan realized that a solid foundation was the first place to start in defining a meaningful life. He recognized the importance of position, purpose, passion, perspective, and priorities in life. All of these concepts linked together perfectly and gave him a platform to teach his children lessons about what really matters most.

A few years ago Dan had lunch with his friend Alex and shared some of the concepts he learned about life in his Bible study. His friend encouraged Dan to write these down not only as a lesson for his children but for others to read. Dan didn't consider himself much of an author, but he thought it was a good idea. He began to write, and it became the book you are reading right now. His full name is Steven Dan Dapper. He is just an ordinary guy, serving an extraordinary God on the journey of life beyond living.

THE CONCLUSION
OF THE MATTER

The concepts in this book are a starting point to defining life. Once you have defined your life in principle, position, and purpose, you must then determine your direction. Answering five critical life questions will help you define where you are and determine where you need to go.

WHAT DO YOU BELIEVE?

This question relates to principle. What do you believe about God, life, family, morals, ethics, fate, and relationships? Only you can answer this question. The journey of life requires that you define your beliefs in these areas and refine them as you mature. The answer to this question will set a precedent for your decisions and your values. The answer to this question will determine the type of legacy you leave and the magnitude of impact you will have on others.

WHY DO YOU BELIEVE WHAT YOU BELIEVE?

What are your beliefs based on? Once you investigate the source of your beliefs, you can compare the source of your belief system to the requirements of a solid principle provided in this book. You may need to change your principle after reading this. You may need to spend more time studying your principle so you know why you believe what you believe. If you need to make changes, make them now. If making changes requires effort, then develop a plan and execute against that plan. Each person is accountable for his or her own life. Take accountability for yours.

WHAT IS YOUR PURPOSE?

Once you know what your principle is and you know why you believe what you believe, you need to use that knowledge to drive your purpose. You are here for a reason. You are reading this book for a reason. Only you can take accountability for your own life. Only you can ensure that you have a meaningful impact on the world. William Shakespeare wrote, "Be not afraid of greatness: some are born great, some achieve greatness and some have greatness thrust upon them." Most people are not born great, nor do they have greatness thrust upon them. For most the responsibility is to achieve greatness by fulfilling purpose. You must own defining your purpose, and you must own fulfilling your purpose.

WHERE ARE YOU?

This question defines your position. Where are you physically, spiritually, emotionally, mentally, morally, and relationally? Because life is a journey, you may not be exactly where you want to be in one or more of these areas, but before you can determine where you want to go, you must first know where you are. I have a GPS I use when I travel. No matter what address I type into the unit, the GPS cannot instruct me on how to get to my destination until it first determines where I am. The same is true with your life. Know your position in each of the dimensions discussed in this book. Defining position is the first step toward maturity.

WHERE DO YOU WANT TO BE?

This question also relates to position but in the future tense. Take time to determine what type of legacy you want to leave. Take time to commit to becoming the type of man or woman you want to be. No child ever wants to grow up to be an alcoholic or a lonely miser. Too often people find themselves in bad situations because of bad choices. You must have a goal and a plan to get there. The path to get where you want to be in life requires that you know where you are and then that you develop a plan to get to where you want to be. Once you have defined your position on every level and you know where you want to go, the next step is a plan to get you there. Compare where you are and where you want to be. What are the gaps? What is missing in your life? What character traits do you need to work on to be better? You own your improvement plan.

When you have answered these questions for your-self, you should have a good understanding of what you need to change. You should know where you have areas you need to work on in order to leave the legacy you want to leave. The next step is of upmost importance—have a plan. A plan is more than just acknowledging where you are. A good plan details where you want to be, and it details how to get there. Your plan should include milestone events and the input of people who can hold you accountable. Improvement is a continuing process that takes a lot of work, but leaving a legacy for those behind you and impacting lives is priceless. The next step is yours. What will you do with this information? What legacy will you leave?

It all comes down to this:

For God so loved the world that he gave his one and only Son, that whosoever believes in him shall not perish but have eternal life. (John 3:16)

The thief comes only to steal and kill and destroy; I have come that they may have life, and have it to the full. (John 10:10)

Jesus answered, "I am the way and the truth and the life. No one comes to the Father except through me." (John 14:6)

This day I call heaven and earth as witnesses against you that I have set before you life and death, blessings and curses. Now choose life, so that you and your children may live and that you may love the LORD you God, listen to his voice, and hold fast to him. (Deut. 30:19–20)

The choice is yours.
Choose life.

NOTES

1. Charles F. Horne, *The Code of Hammurabi* (London: Forgotten Books, 2007).

2. Russell Ash, *The Top Ten of Everything 2003* (London: DK Adult, 2002).

3. John MacArthur, *The MacArthur Bible Commentary* (Nashville: Thomas Nelson, 2005).

4. See http://articles.cnn.com/2009/mar/09.

5. F. F. Bruce, *Israel and the Nations: The History of Israel from the Exodus to the Fall of the Second Temple* (Westmont, IL: IVP Academic, 1998).

6. See www.blueletterbible.org.